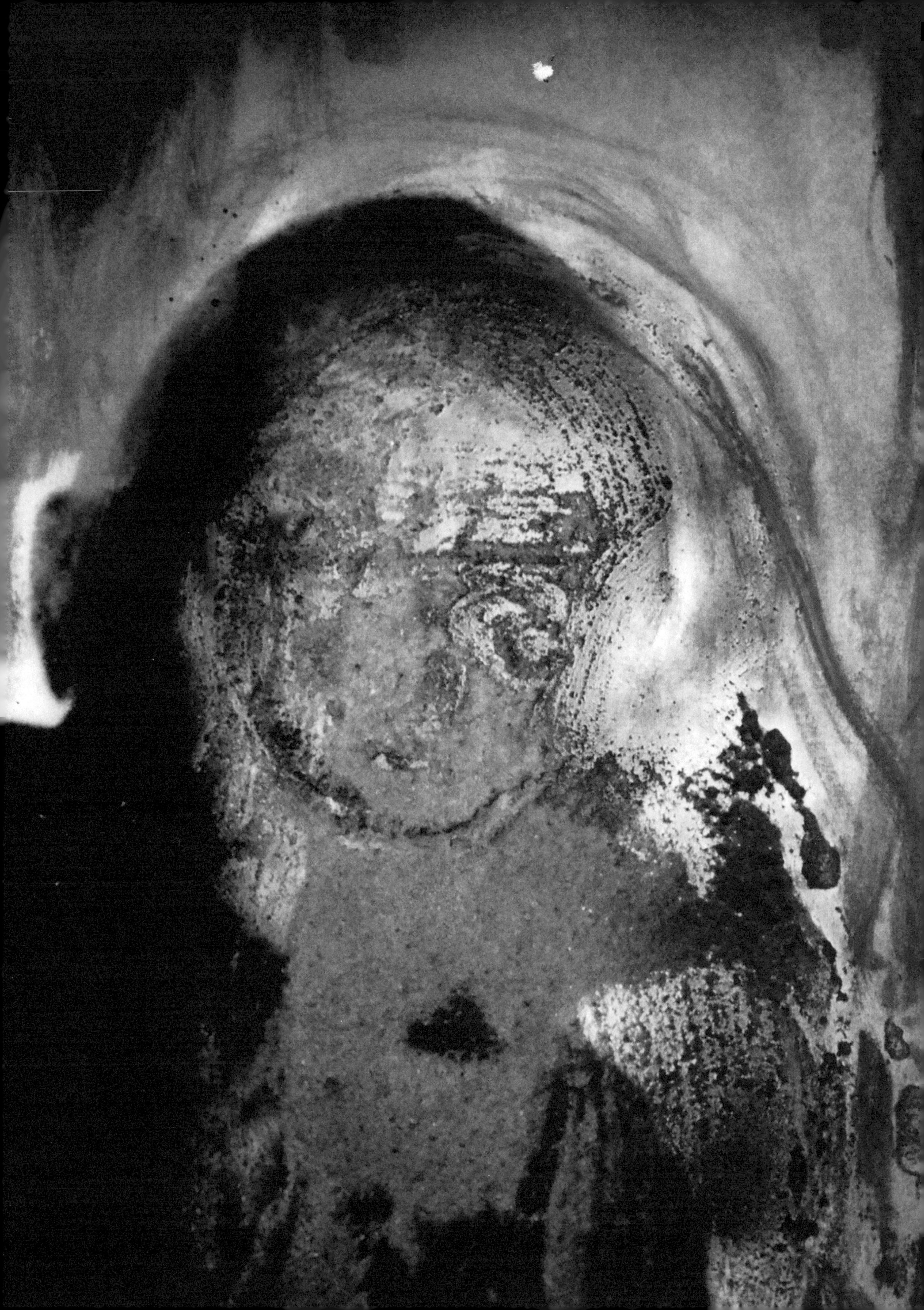

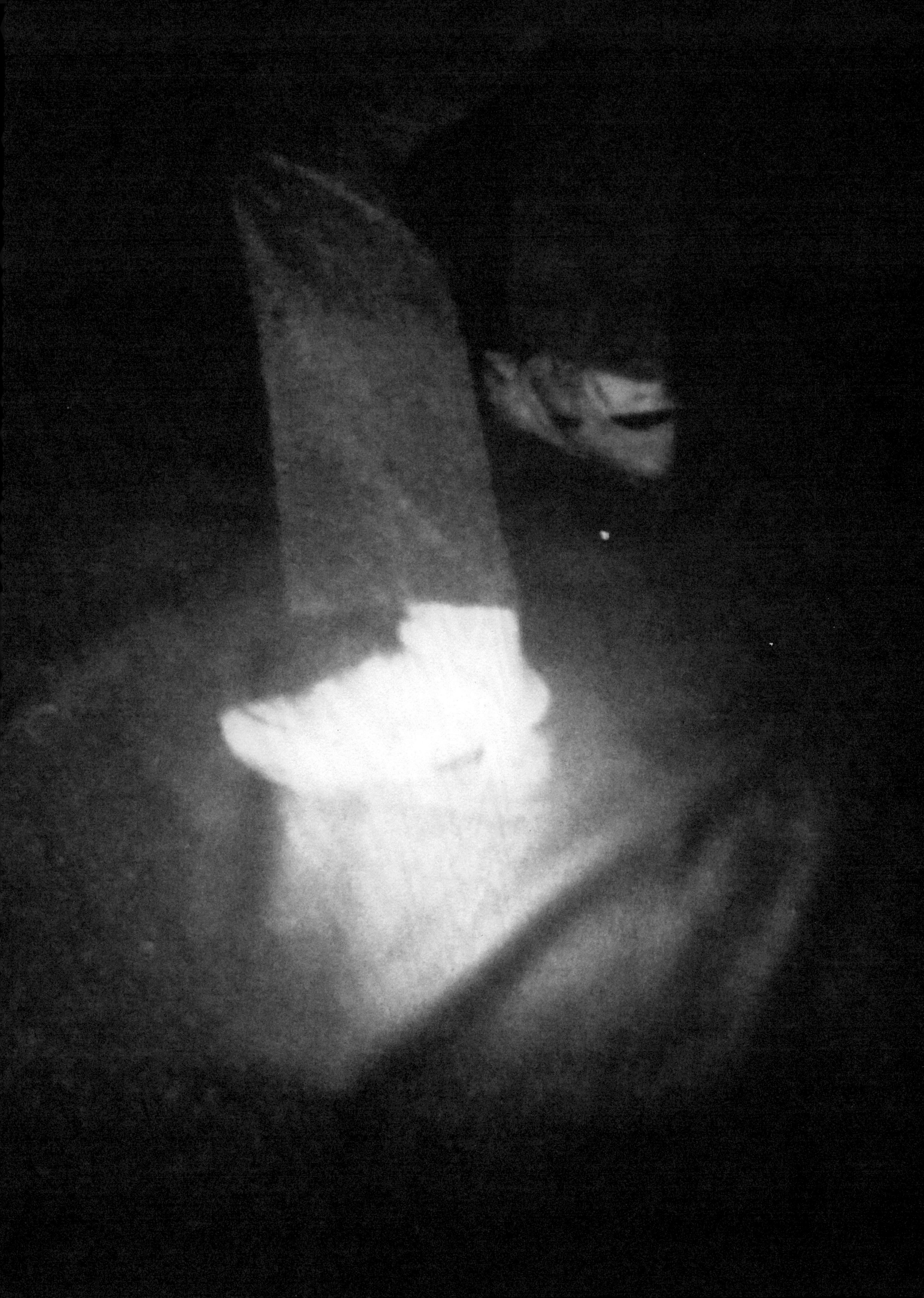

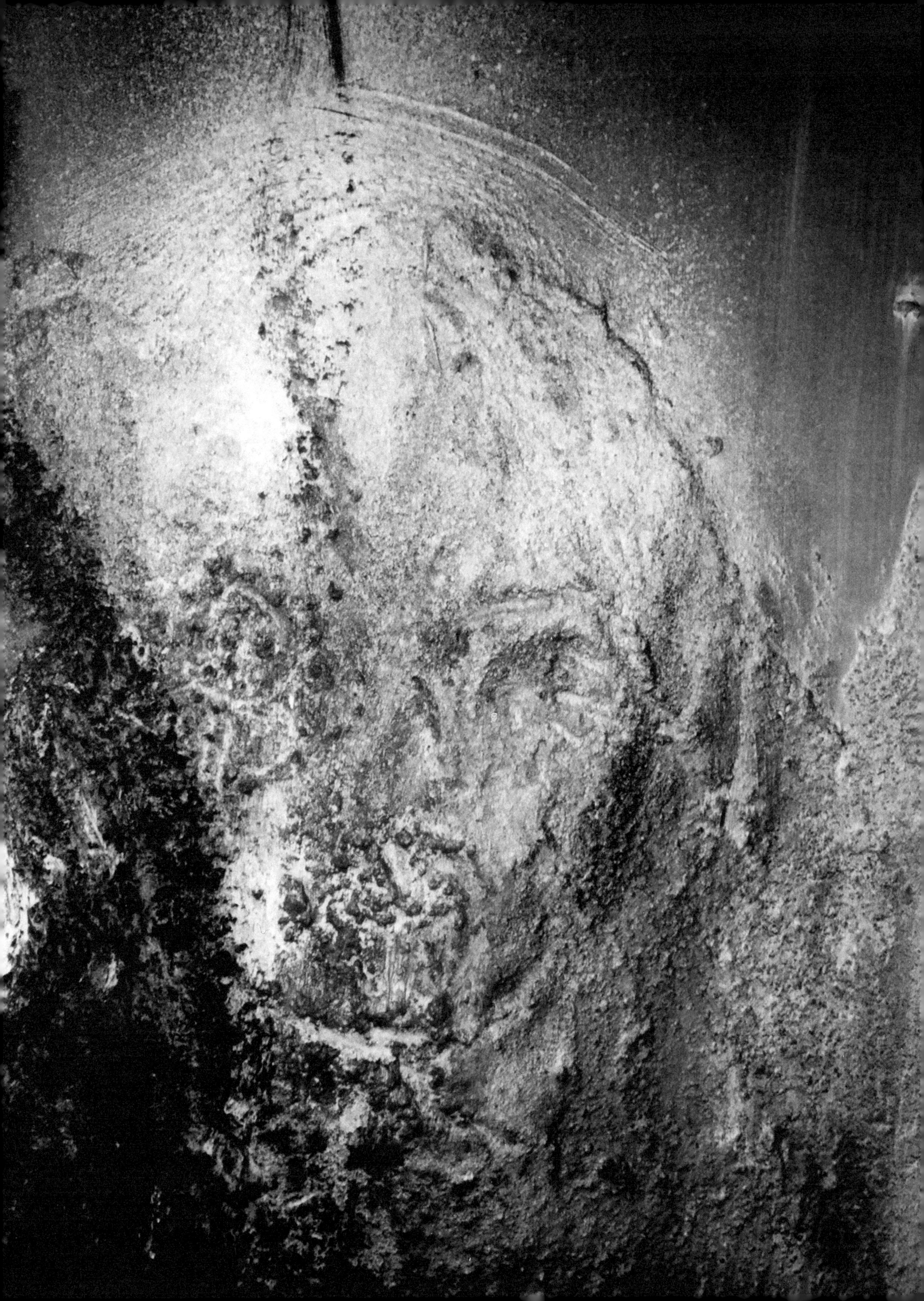

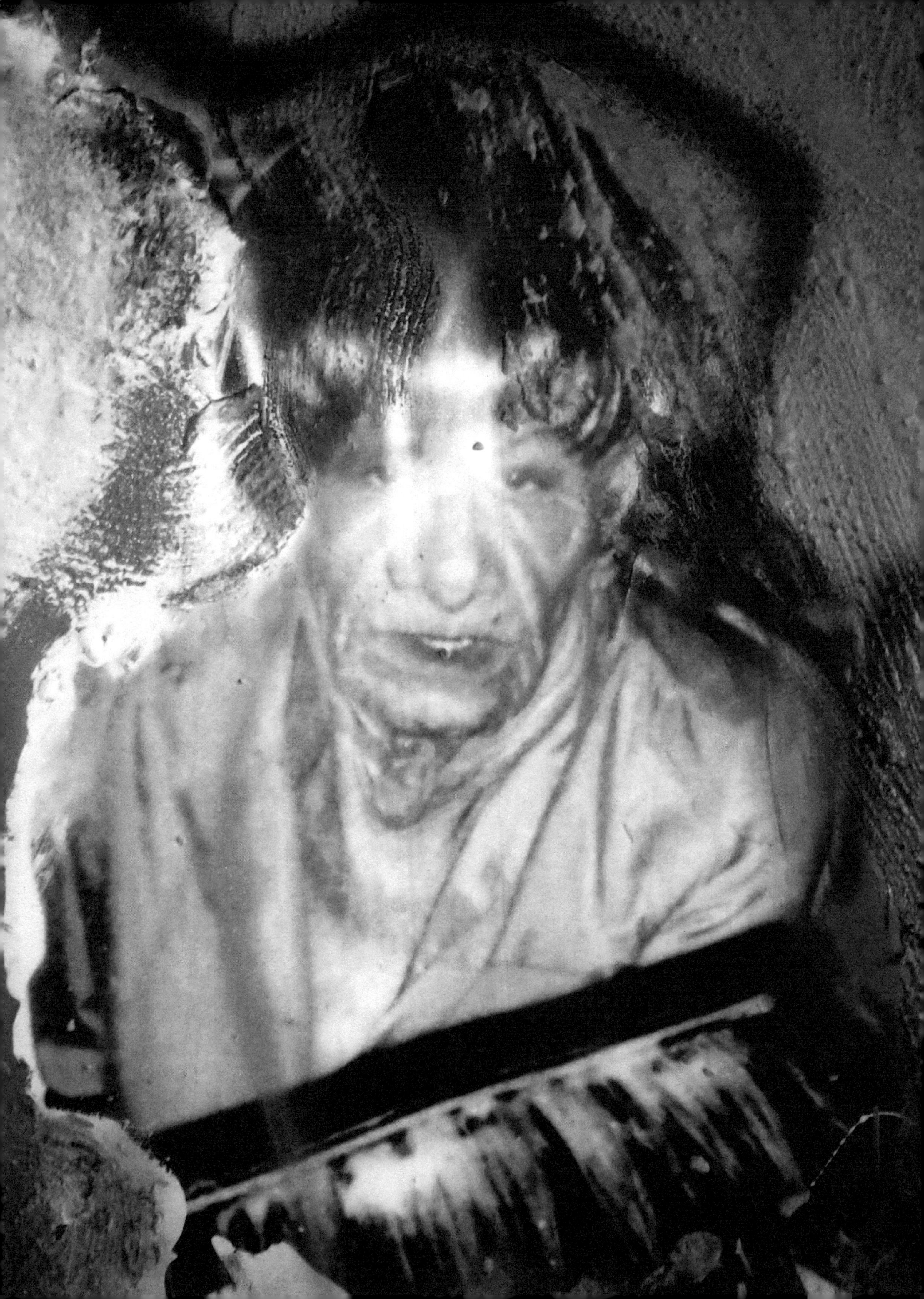

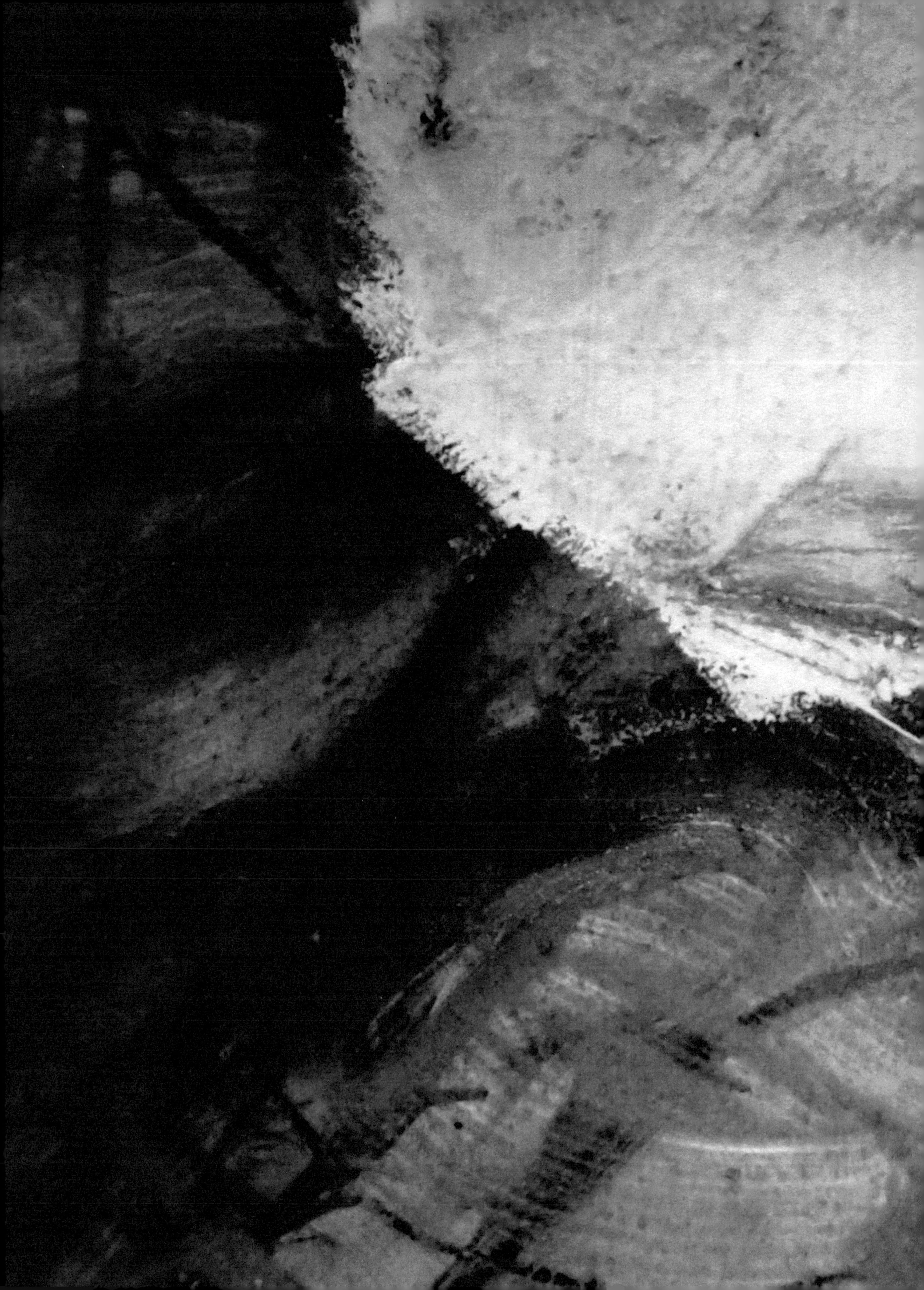

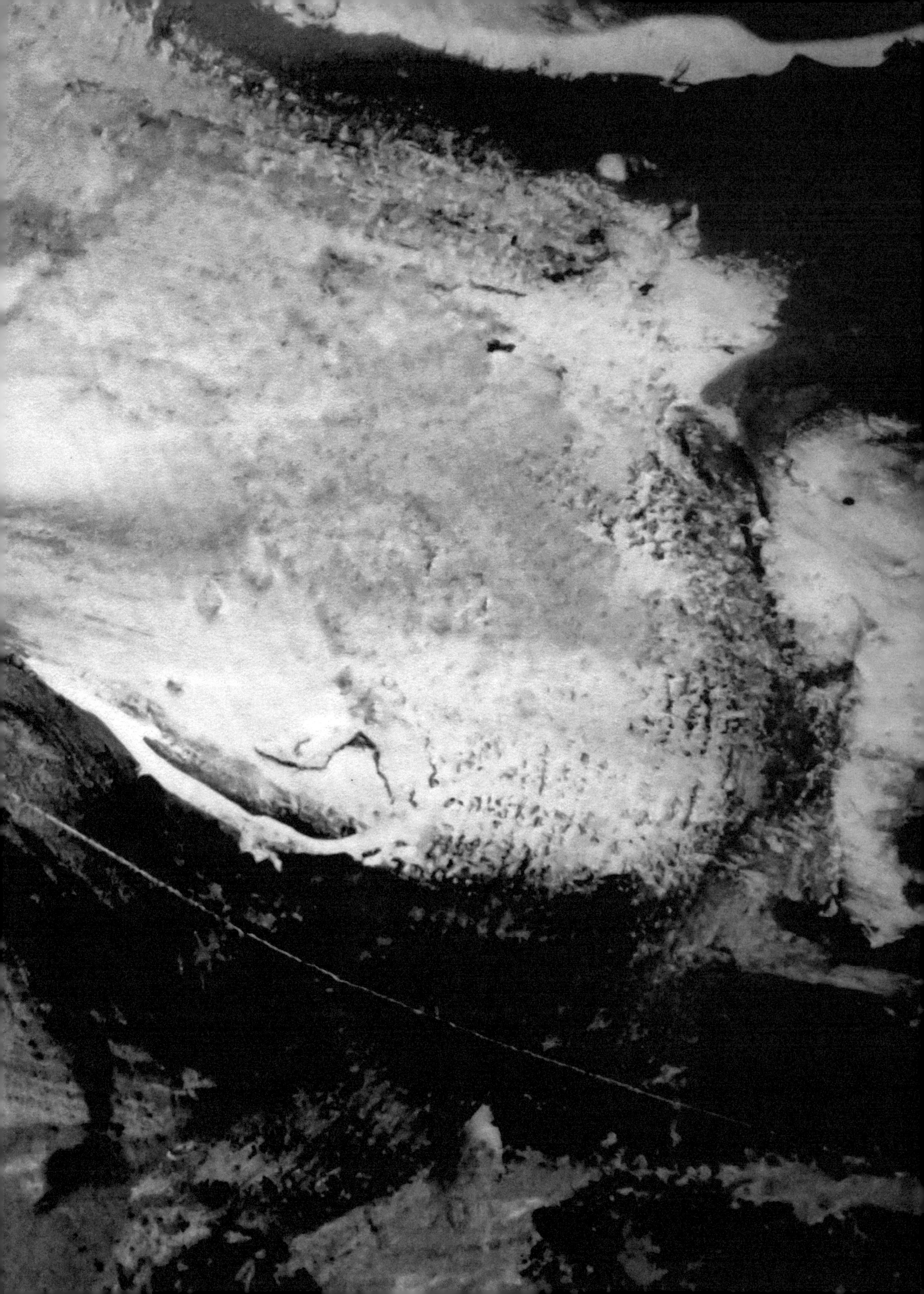

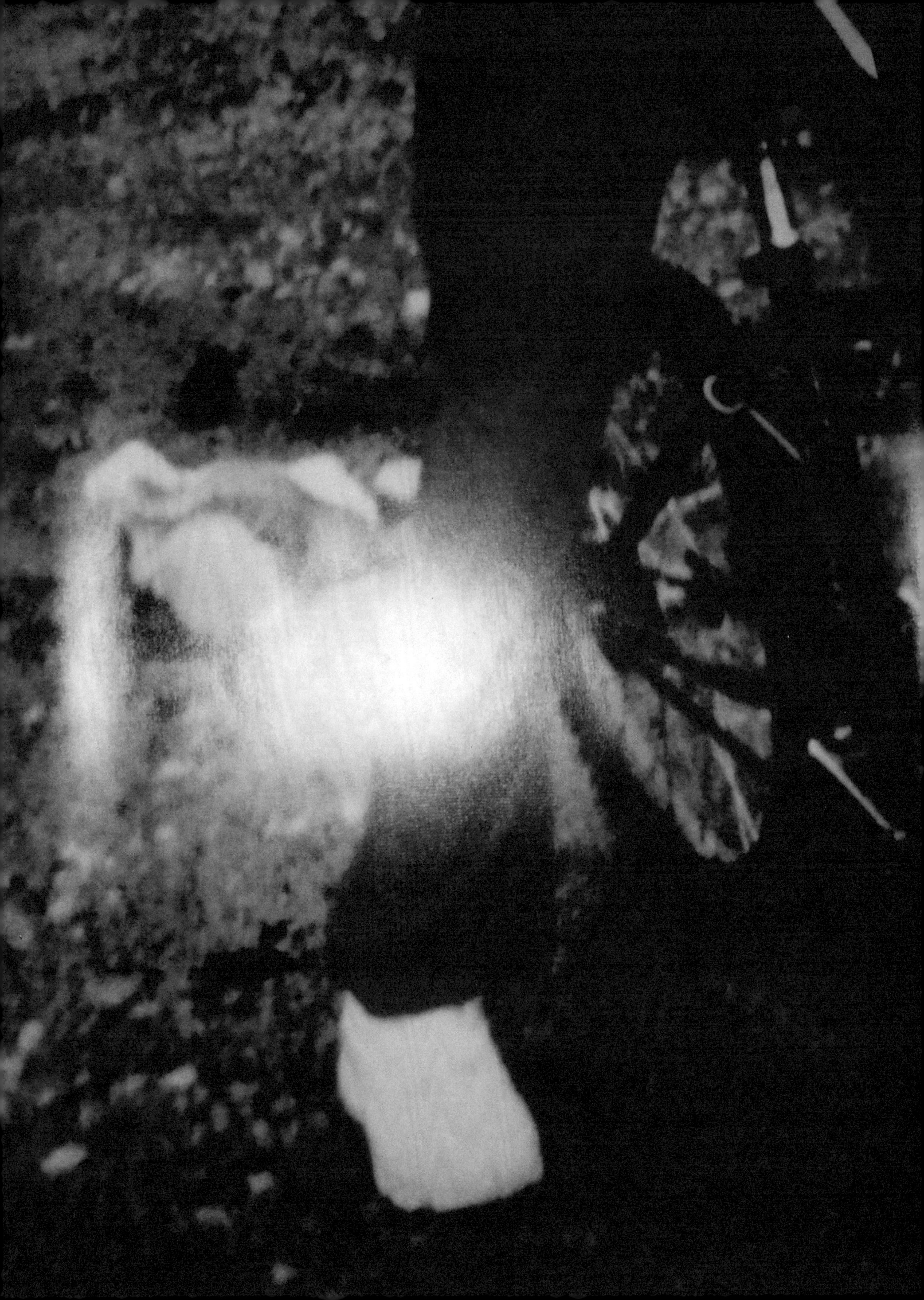

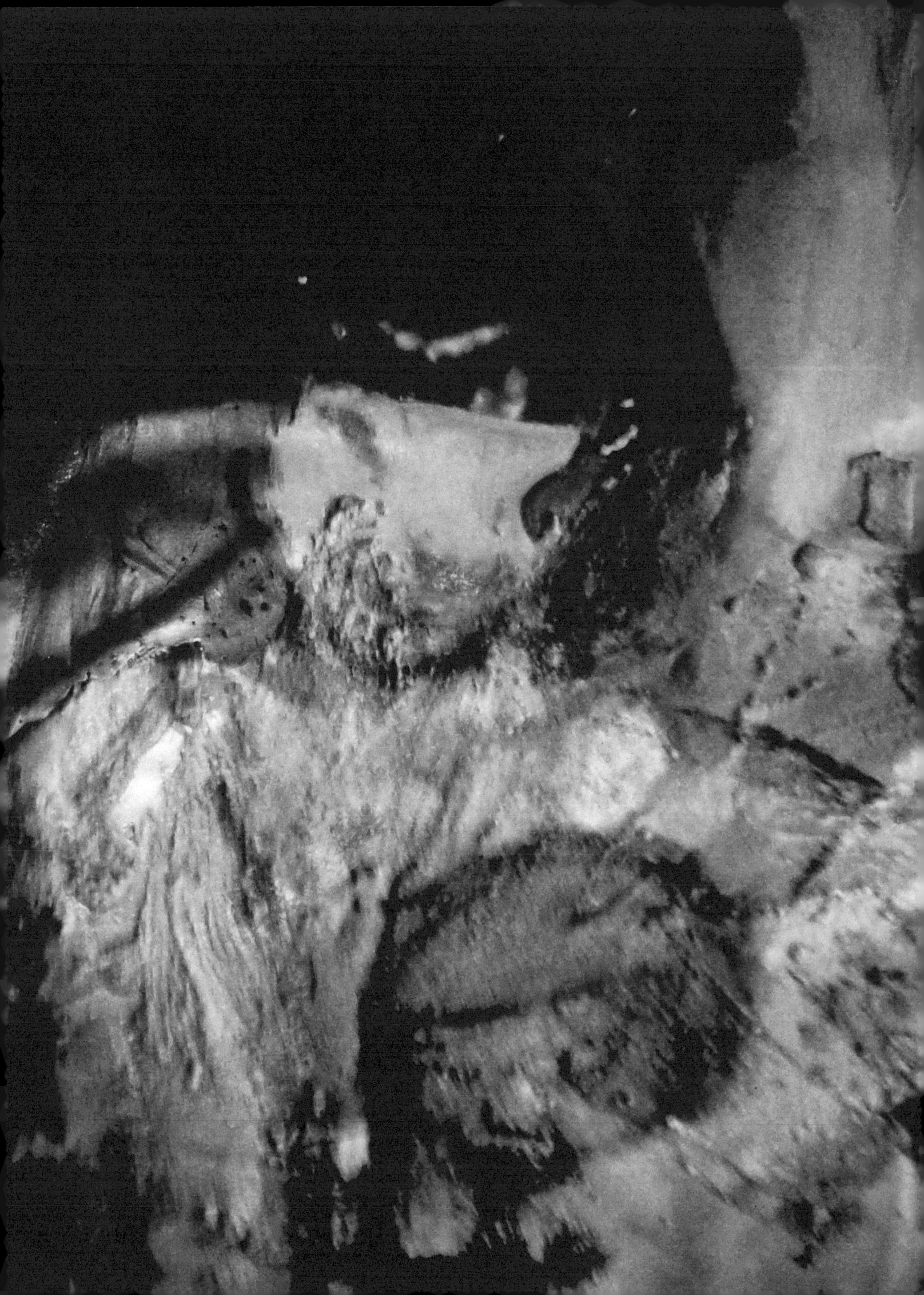

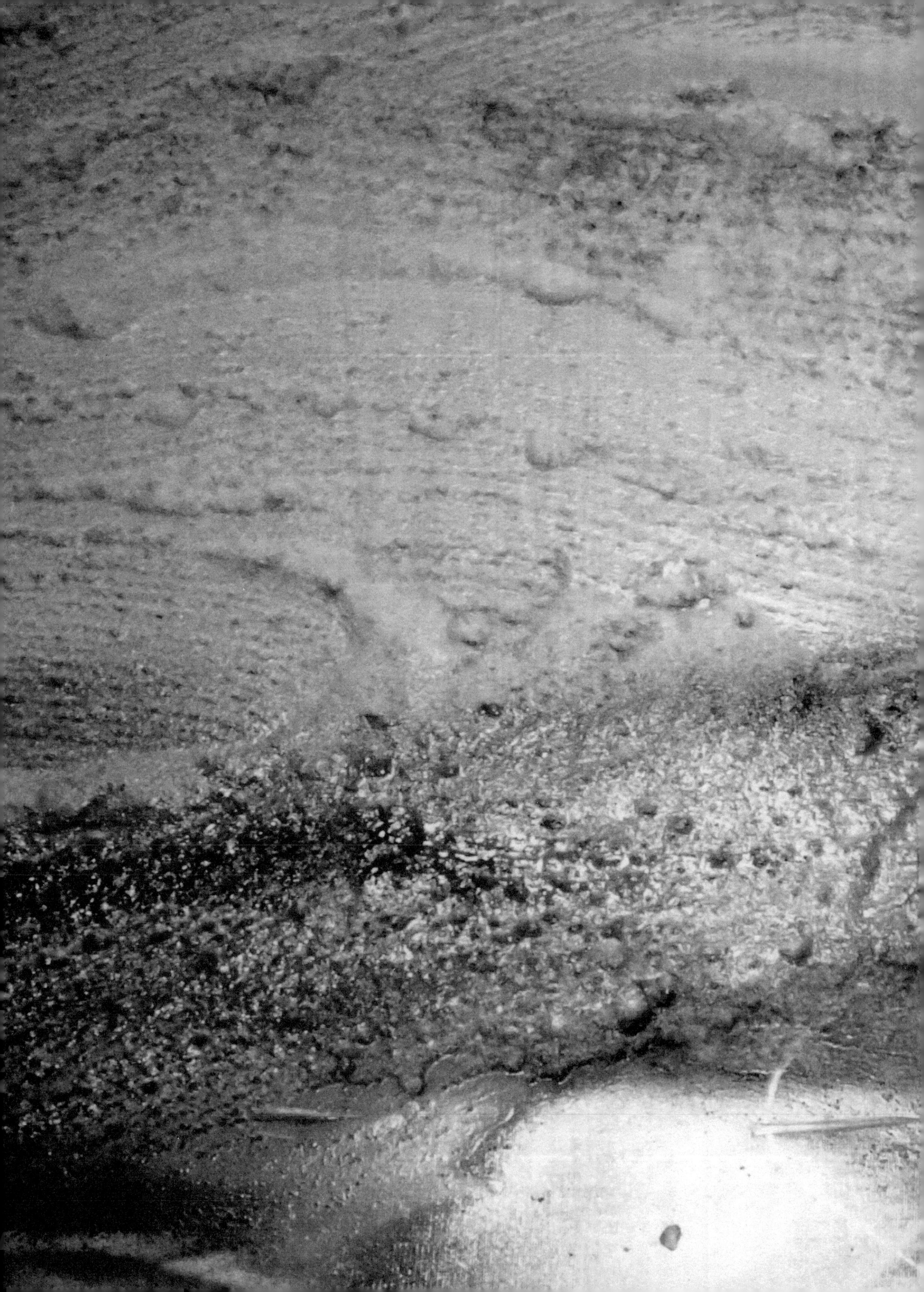

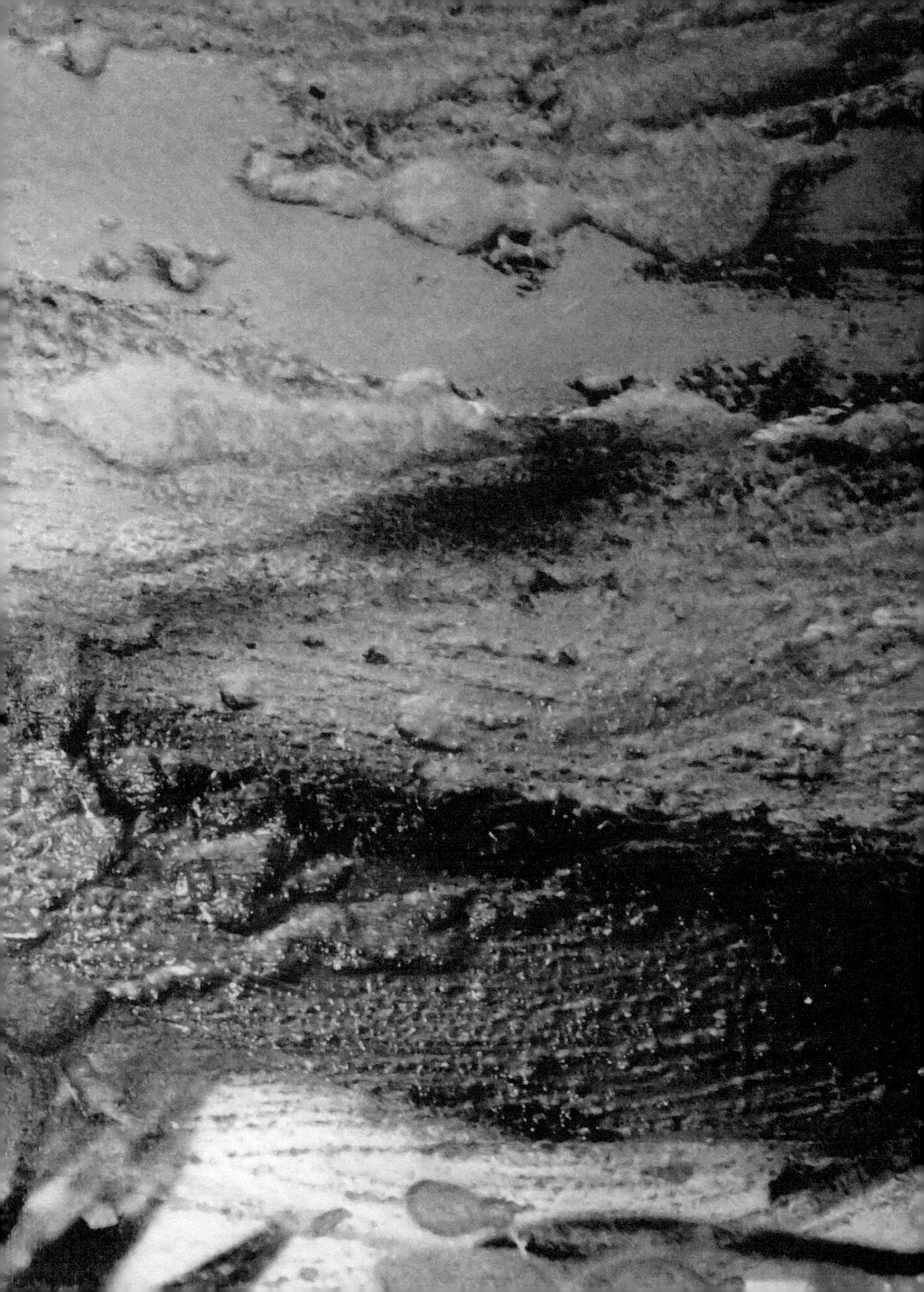

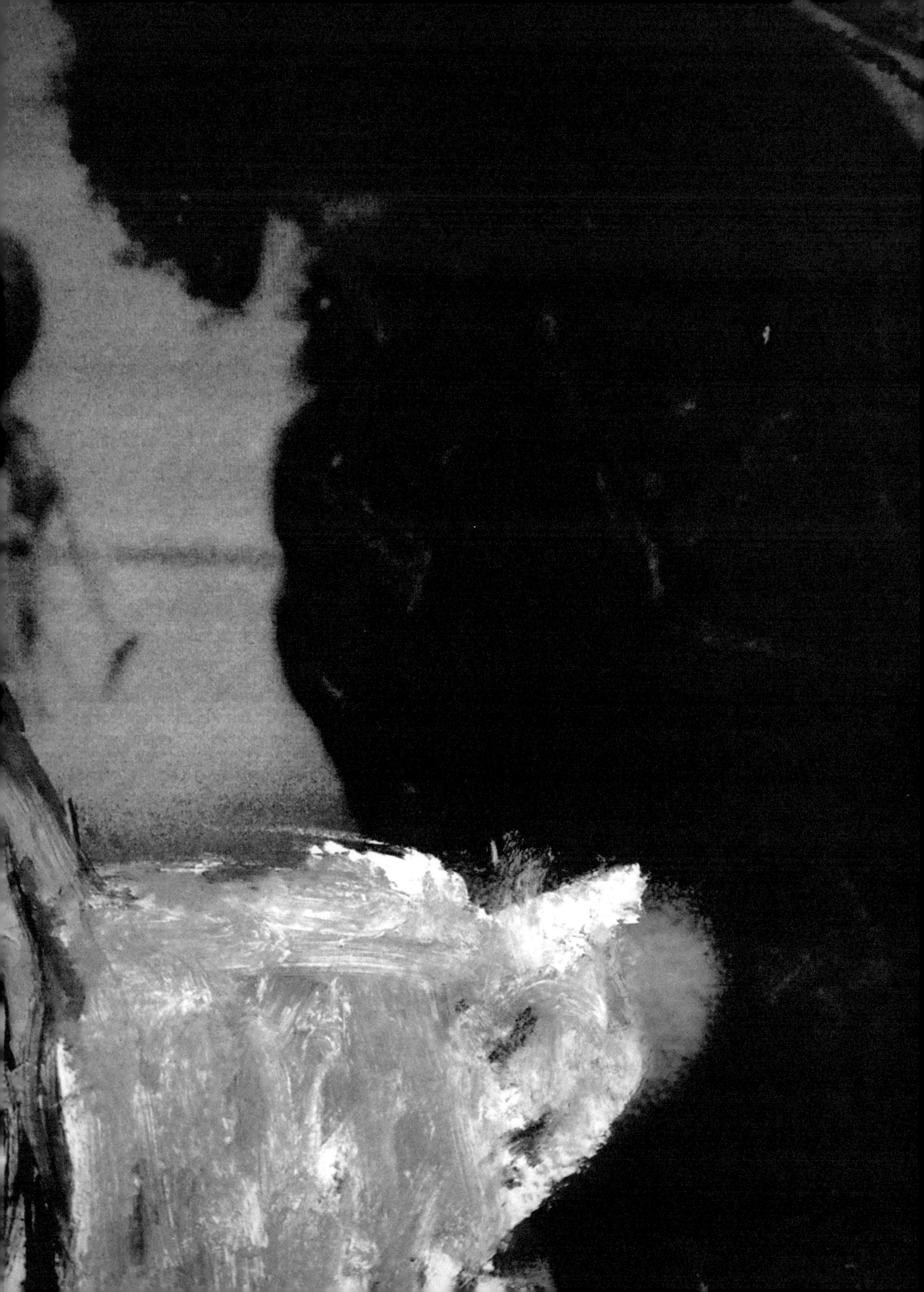

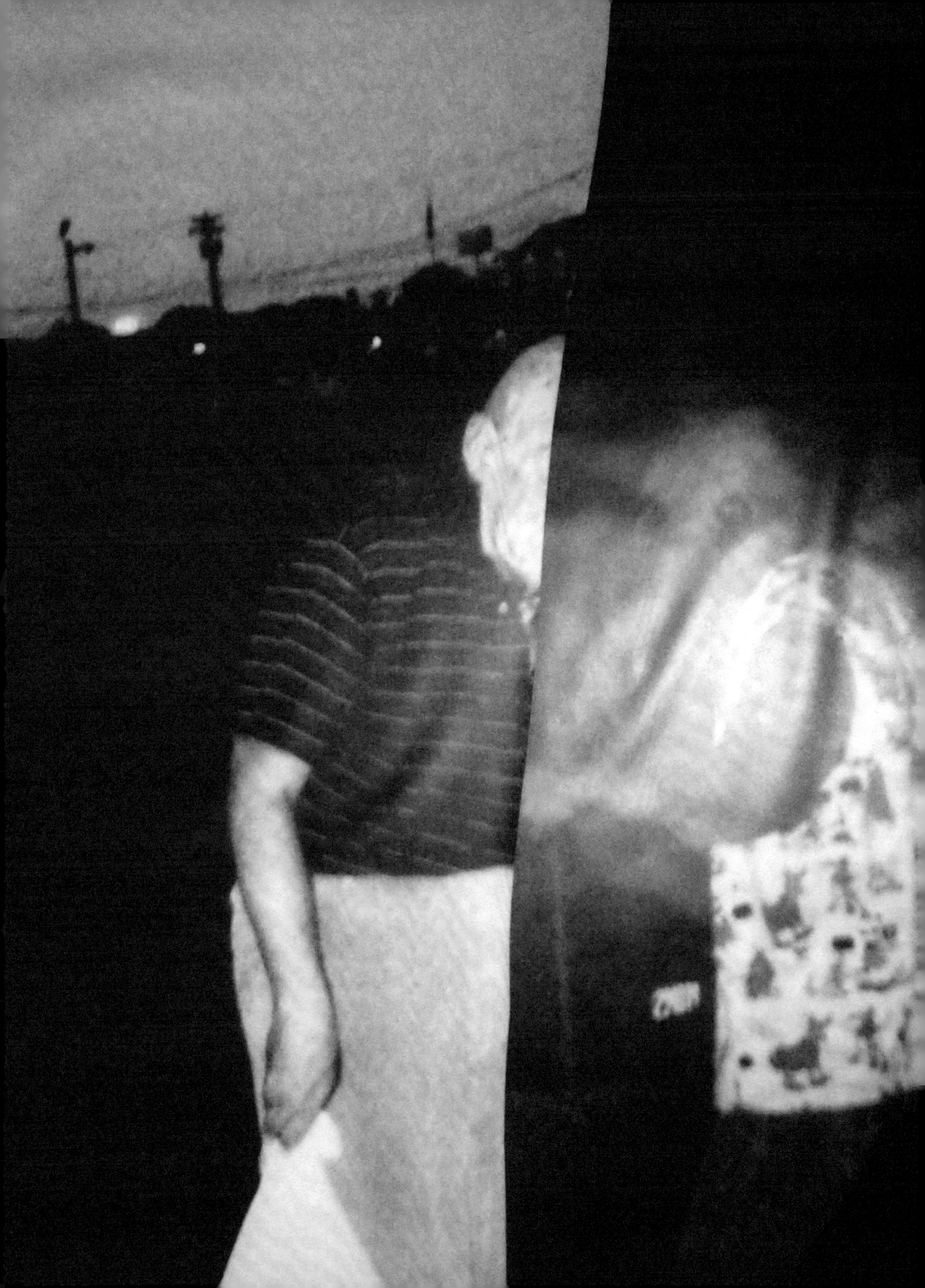

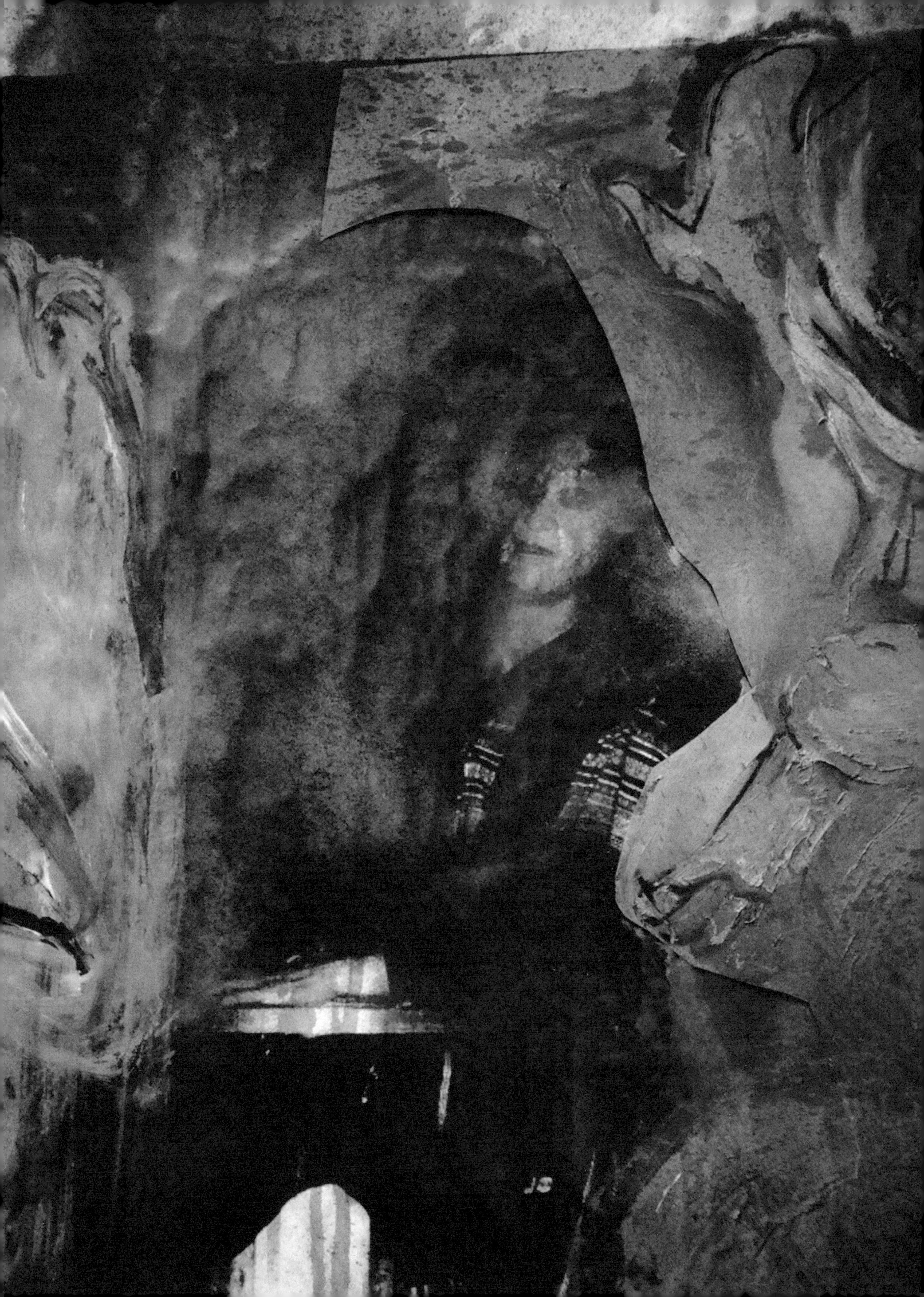

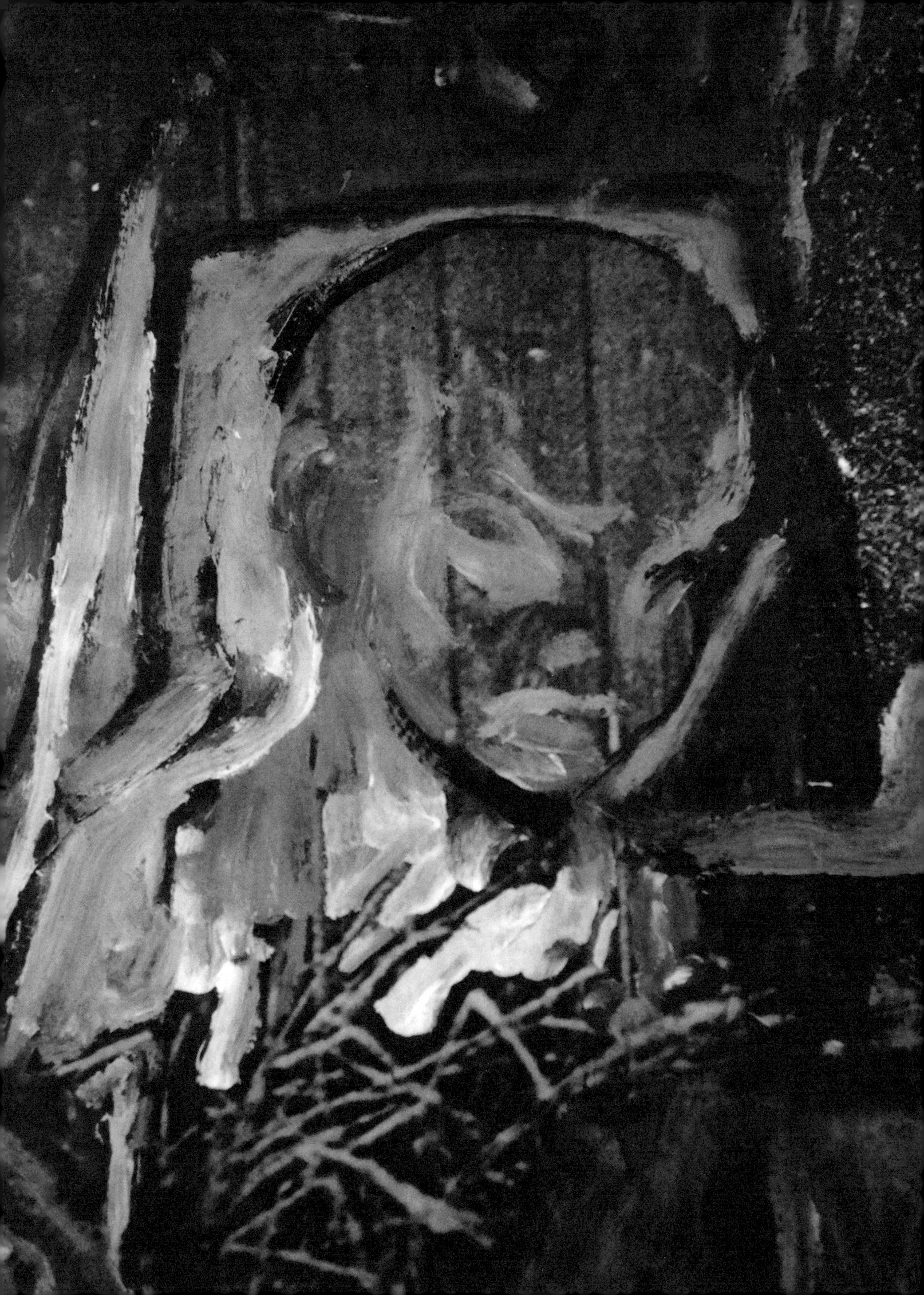

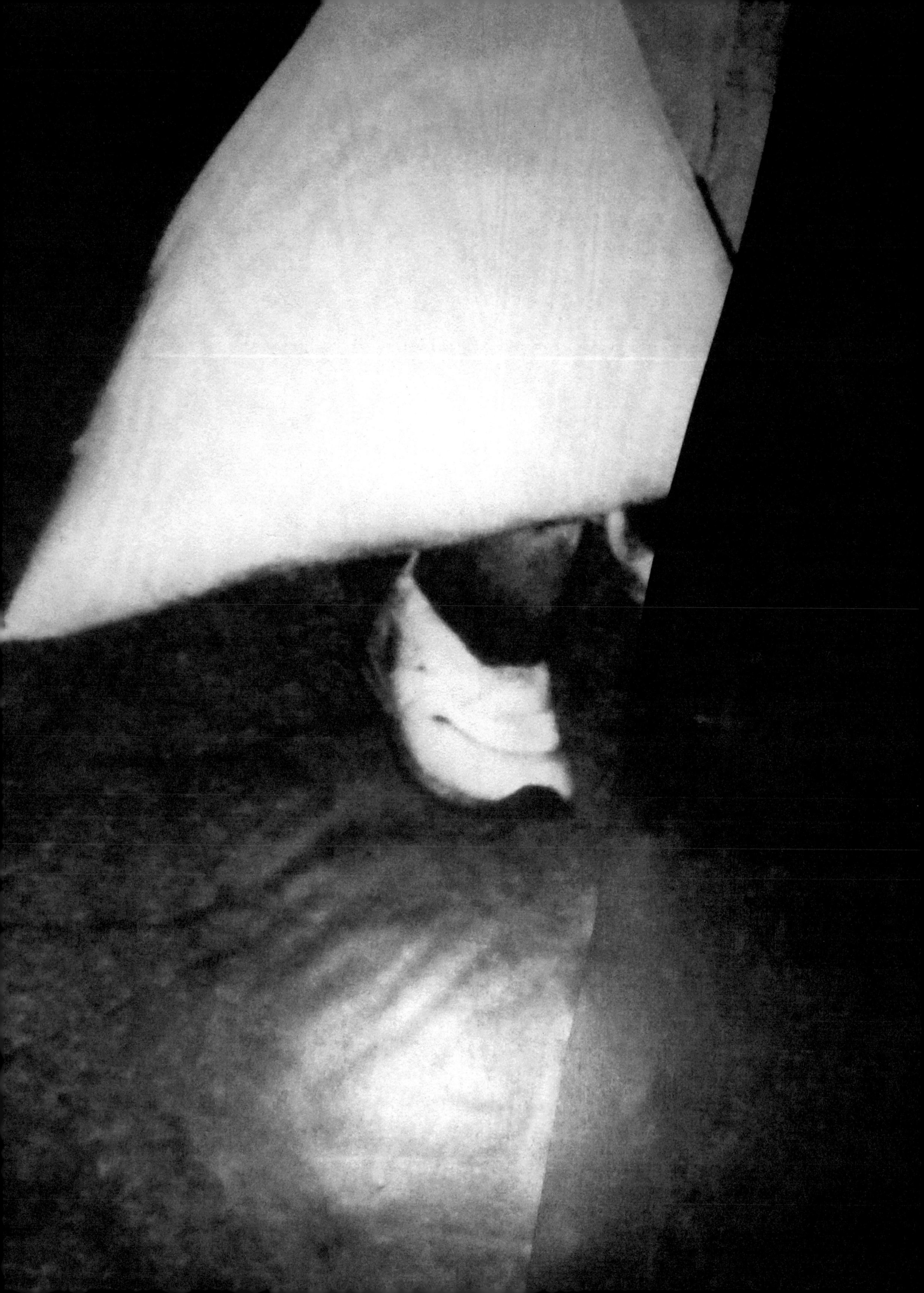

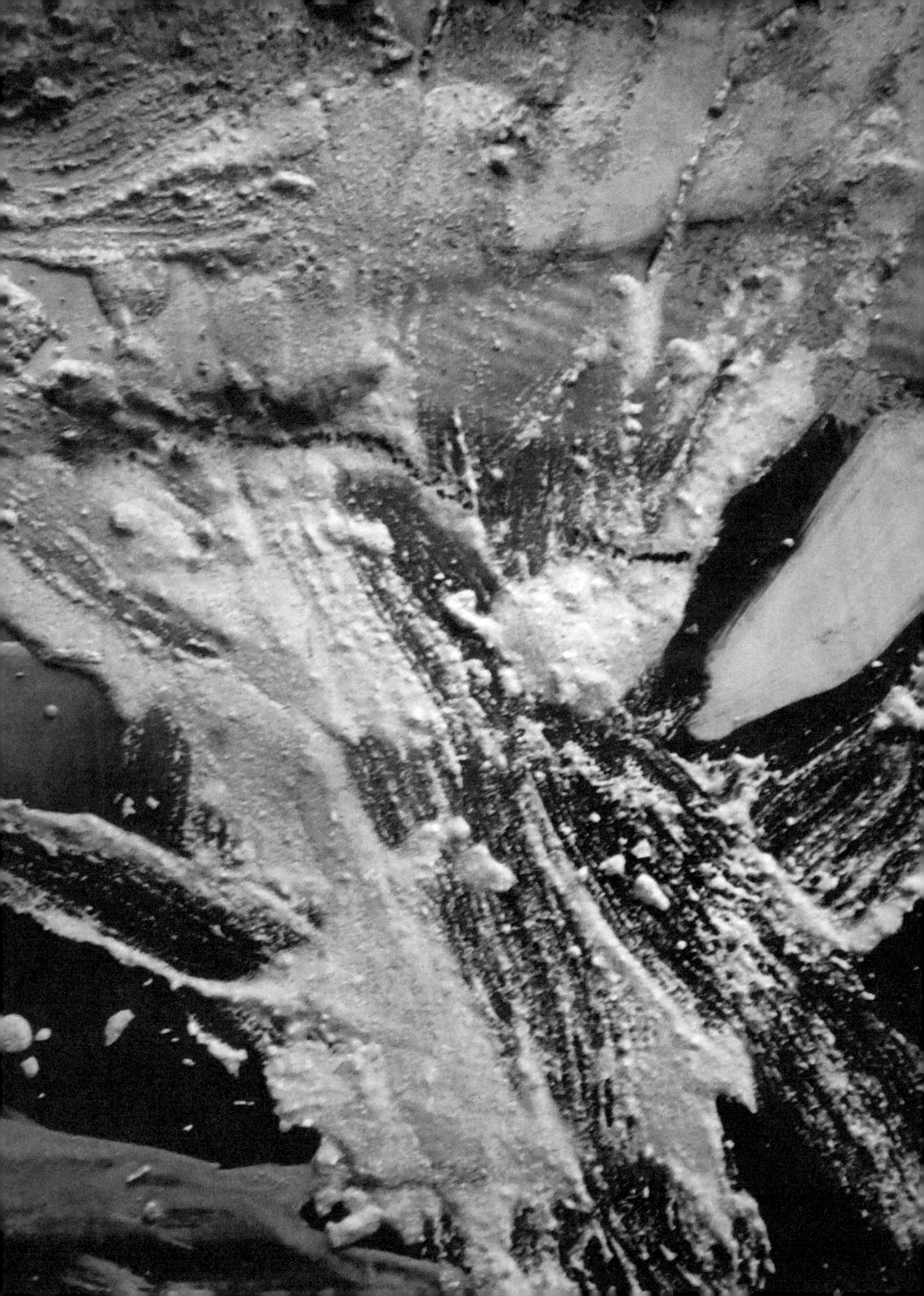

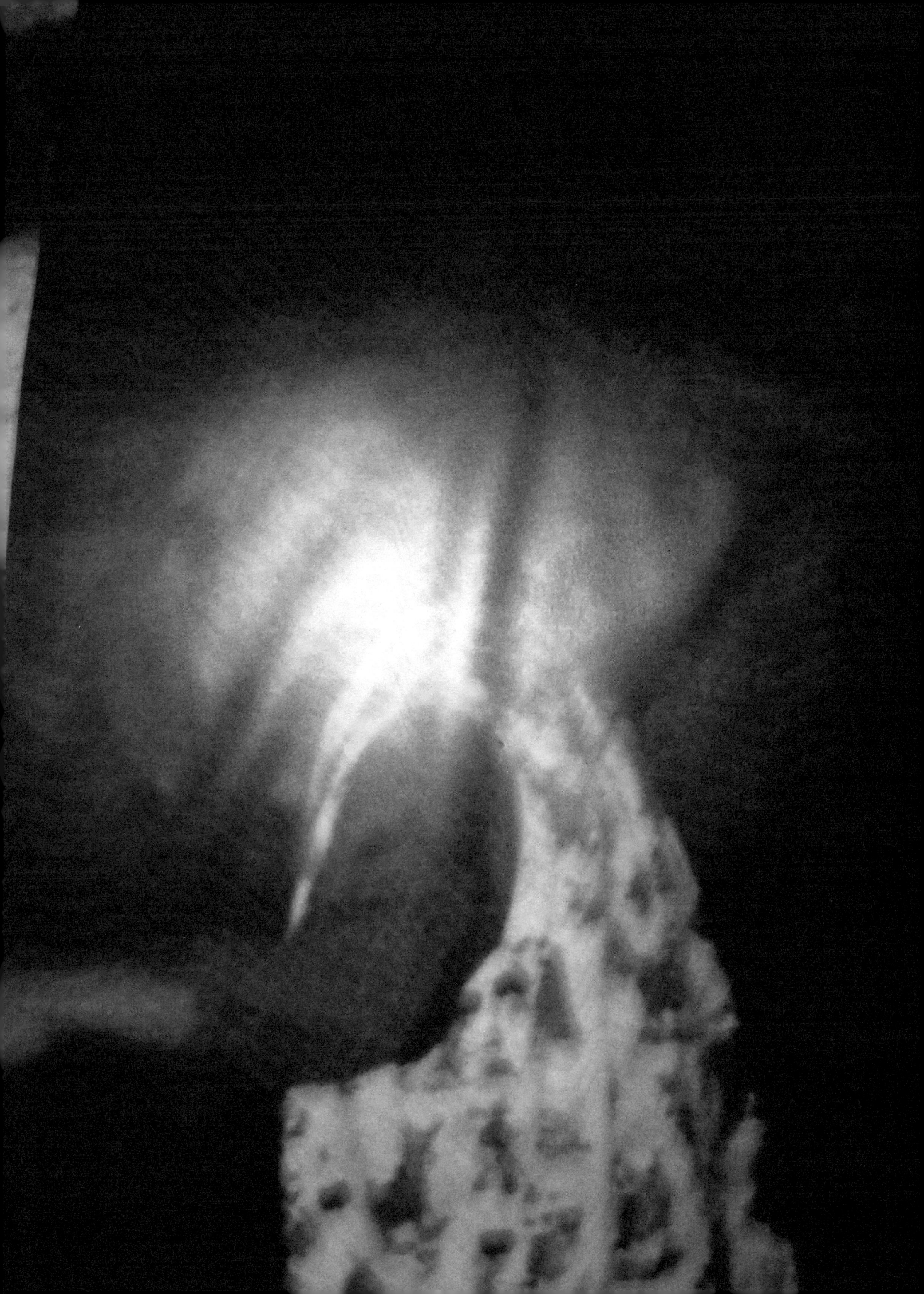

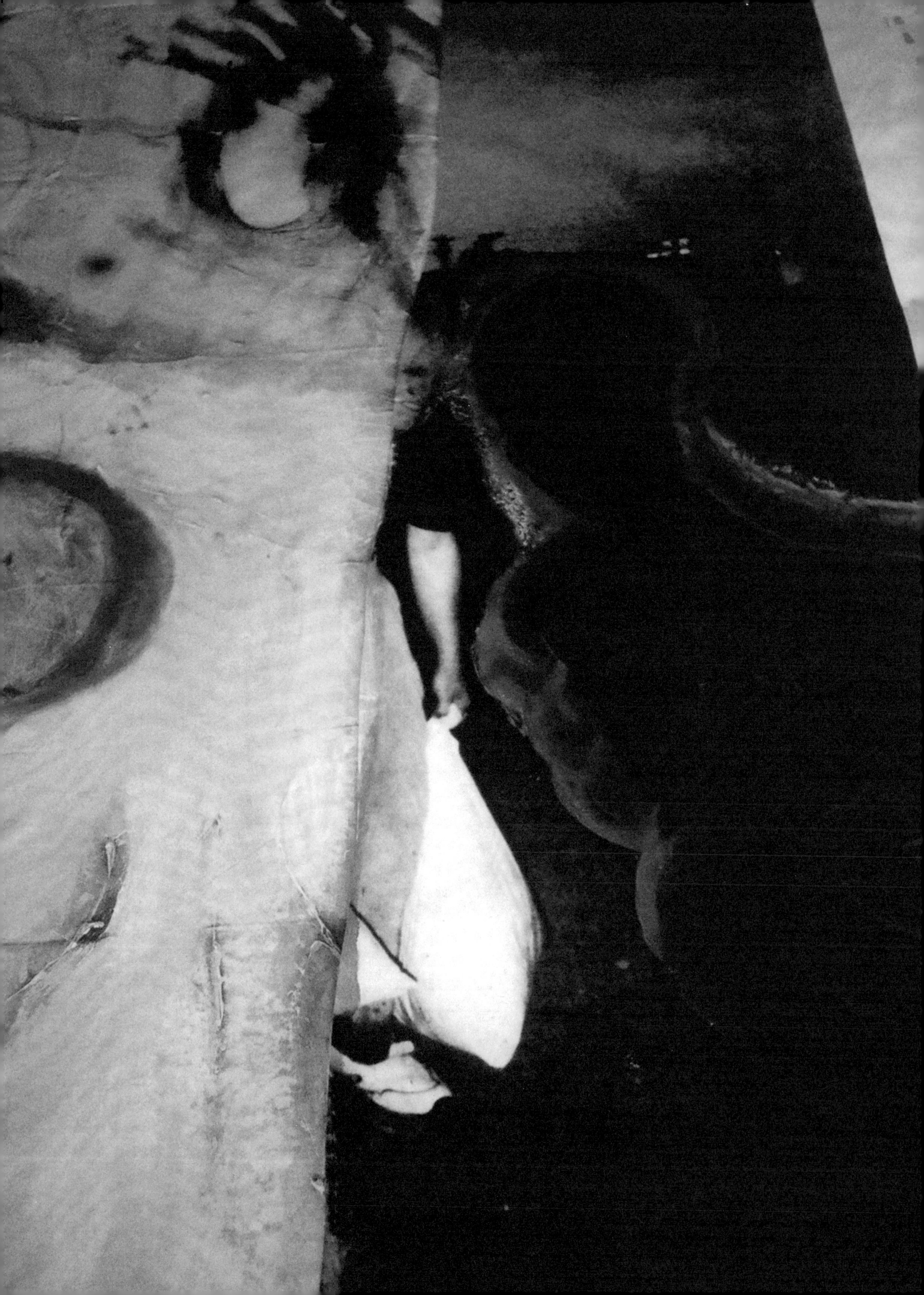

Published in conjunction with the exhibition
"Shadow Fux"
Curated by Gianni Jetzer
Swiss Institute Contemporary Art, New York
November 24, 2010–January 30, 2011

CATALOGUE

Published by the agnès b. Endowment Fund and
Swiss Institute Contemporary Art
Editor: Gianni Jetzer
Editorial Coordination: Piper Marshall
Authors: Antoine Catala, Richard Flood, Gianni Jetzer, Piper Marshall, Cameron Shaw
Copy Editing: Stephen Braren, Polly Watson
Graphic Design: Li, Inc.
Printed in Italy

INSTITUTION

Swiss Institute Contemporary Art
495 Broadway, 3rd Floor, New York, NY 10012
+1 212 925 2035
info@swissinstitute.net
swissinstitute.net

THANK YOU

Charles-Marie Anthonioz, agnès b., Stanley Buchthal,
Antoine Catala, Bonnie Clearwater, Peter Doig, Richard Flood, Dan Graham,
Maja Hoffmann, Peter Kilchmann, Lefty Korine, Rachel Korine, Patrick Li,
Parinaz Mogadassi, Marc Payot, Andrea Rosen, Cameron Shaw, Bettina Sorg,
Charline von Heyl, Olivier Zahm, Seth Zucker

DISTRIBUTION

France:
Les presses du réel
35 rue Colson, 21000 Dijon, France
+33 (0) 380307523
info@lespressesdureel.com
lespressesdureel.com

North America:
D.A.P. Distributed Art Publishers
155 Sixth Avenue, New York, NY 10013
+1 212 627 1999
dap@dapinc.com
artbook.com

ISBN: 978-2-906496-59-0 (FRANCE)
ISBN: 978-1-884692-09-3 (NORTH AMERICA)

SI swiss arts council prohelvetia LUMA FOUNDATION agnès b. endowment fund

SHADOW FUX

Rita Ackermann SHADOW FUX Harmony Korine

bag and hag, 2010
Acrylic medium, spray paint,
enamel, oil on vinyl on canvas
90 x 60 inches
Courtesy of the Artists and
Andrea Rosen Gallery, New York

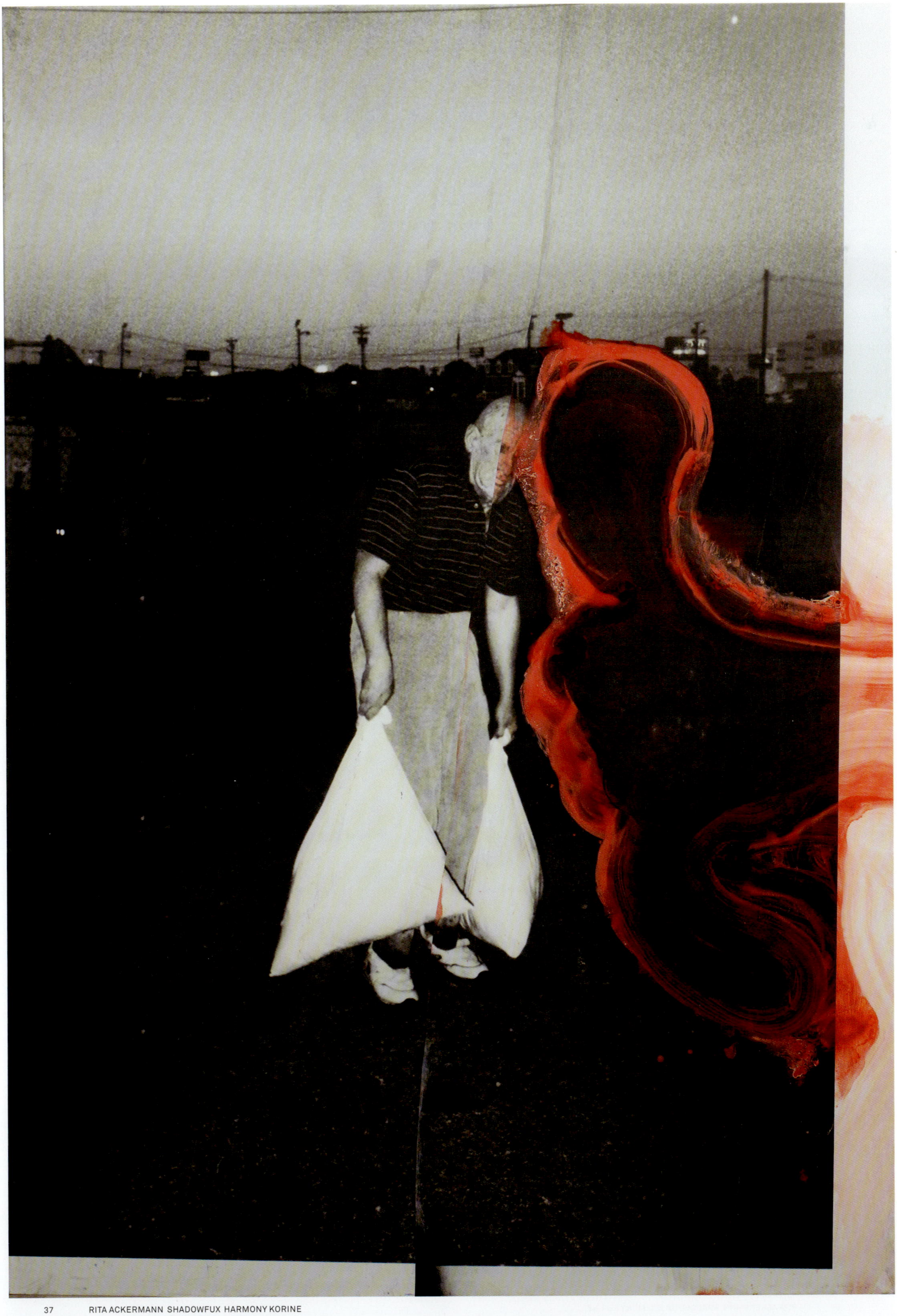

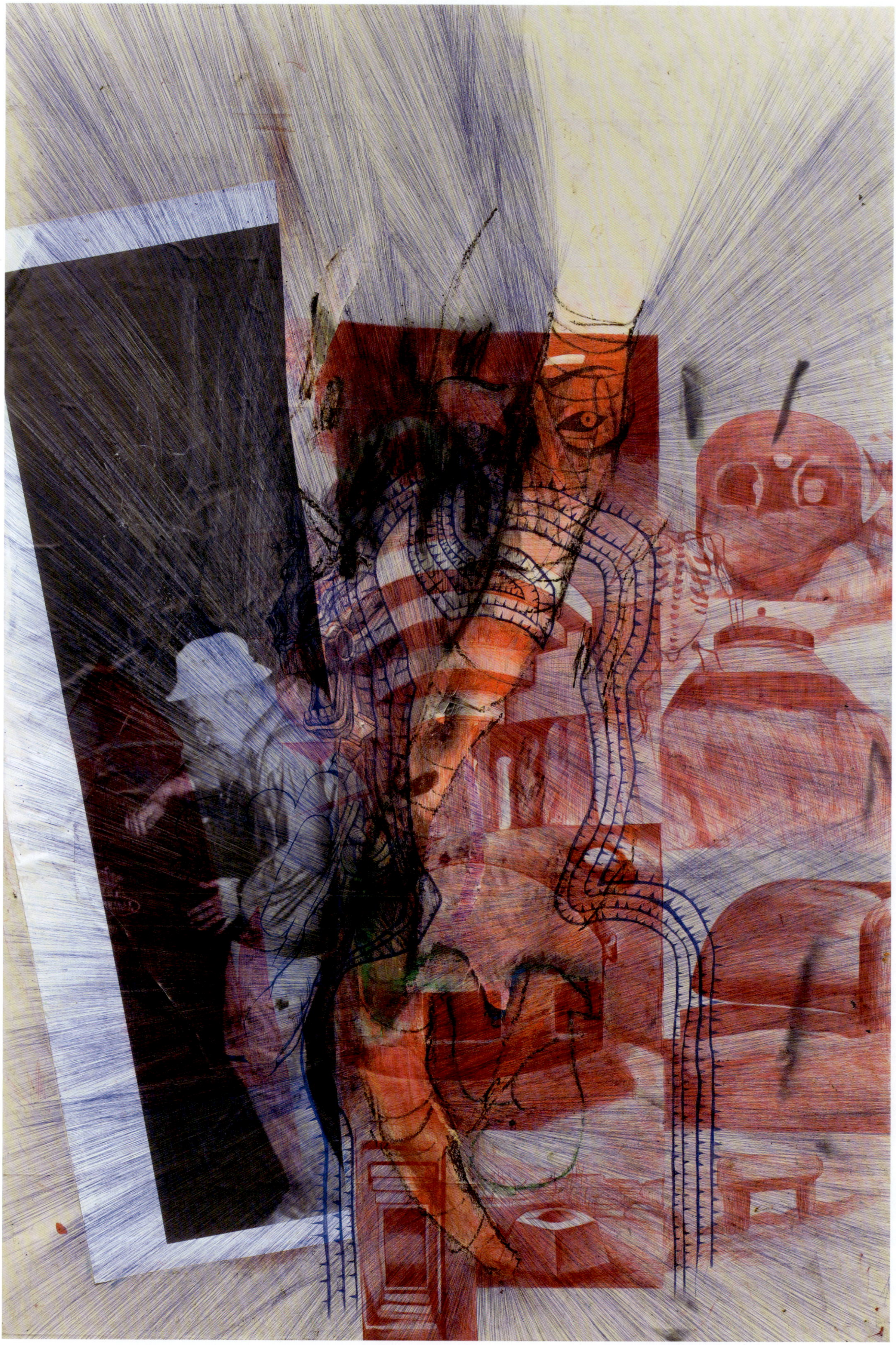

high powered tramps

Gianni Jetzer

Swiss psychologist Jean Piaget records that when he asked a group of children where they thought dreams took place, one of them said that he dreamed in his mouth. If works of art can be compared with dreams at all, *high powered tramps* by Harmony Korine and Rita Ackermann melts like devil's berries in your mouth. The savor is of a feverish kind, something one has never tasted before, elusive and ethereal, warm and cold, unreal yet authentic.

The piece is based on an earlier work by Rita Ackermann entitled *World War III Around My Skull* from 1996–97. Ackermann states that "it was obvious that only World War III could conduct this violent disharmony into an orchestrated piece." While the older piece is entirely covered with color, the recent work seems more composed. With the authority of an altar painting, *high powered tramps* is throned in the middle axis of the exhibition space. Being the only work in the exhibition that is drawn directly on raw canvas, it is in many ways the exception to the rule of the first collaborative show by the two artists. The use of ballpoint pen as an artistic medium further enhances the work's solitary status.

high powered tramps, 2010
Enamel, oil, spray paint, molding paste, ballpoint pen, acrylic medium, vinyl on canvas
110 x 78 inches
Courtesy of the Artists and Andrea Rosen Gallery, New York

The drawing hand, coated with greasy pen pigment, left marks and stains all over the textile surface. The venous blue and arterial red result in a sanguine palette of different shades and grades of oxygen. The loaded red complements the suffocated blue. In between heart and lungs, various characters inhabit the iconic imagery: different bunker-like monuments, massive and introverted; a skull-head apple; an occlusion with pointed dents recalling graphics of battlefields or weather charts; the head of a horse screaming in despair; the melancholic face of a clownish character. All these icons are held together by blue rays of ballpoint, opening up like a fan.

In Paul Virilio's book *Bunker Archeology* (1975)—a copy of which Ackermann keeps in her studio—the French philosopher analyzes the Atlantic Wall fortress bunkers along the French coast in both philosophical and architectural terms, finding astonishing analogies: "A complete series of cultural memories came to mind: the Egyptian mastabas, the Etruscan tombs, the Aztec structures . . . as if this piece of artillery fortification could be identified as a funeral ceremony, as if the Todt Organization could manage only the organization of a religious space . . . " This is also the case with Ackermann and Korine's bunkers and shelters. They are haunted by a nature both bellicose and spiritual. It is often repeated that Friedrich Nietzsche saw a coach driver beating his horse in Italy, threw his arms around the horse in tears, and collapsed. The wide-open eyes of the animal depicted in *high powered tramps* echo this tragic incident.

The demise of a philosopher of Nietzsche's caliber is asking for a symbolic caption that remains in your memory forever.

Belladonna is a plant whose foliage and berries are extremely toxic, containing tropane alkaloids. It has a long history of use as a medicine, cosmetic, and poison. Other names for it—devil's berries, death cherries, deadly nightshade—are poetic. In the past, it was believed that witches used a mixture of belladonna, opium poppies, and other typically poisonous plants in a flying ointment, a tincture they applied to help them fly to gatherings with others.

A rich composition of iconic imagery develops from edge to edge, supported by a large black-and-white sticker introducing a trash humper leaning over, trapped in an exquisite, stubborn astonishment about the absurd fact of his existence. Korine and Ackermann meet and overlap with their shared interest in an unorthodox and mischievous beauty. Central to the praxis of both is the creation of psychologically jarring figures, unsettling presences further enhanced by fragmented narratives.

The works in "Shadow Fux" pair the canvas with the silver screen. The cinema screen is at once shiny, immaculate, untouchable, and sticky with longings. A canvas is more tangible; its irregular woven structure hosts an ensnaring spiderweb of imagery to catch the viewer and induce stories of his or her own. It does not need the effect of the moving image to make the spectator fly as if having dissolved a drop of belladonna in his or her mouth. This candy contains both the image of a dream and a dream image.

<u>bmhex</u>, 2010
Acrylic medium on vinyl
on canvas
90 x 60 inches
Courtesy of the Artists and
Andrea Rosen Gallery, New York

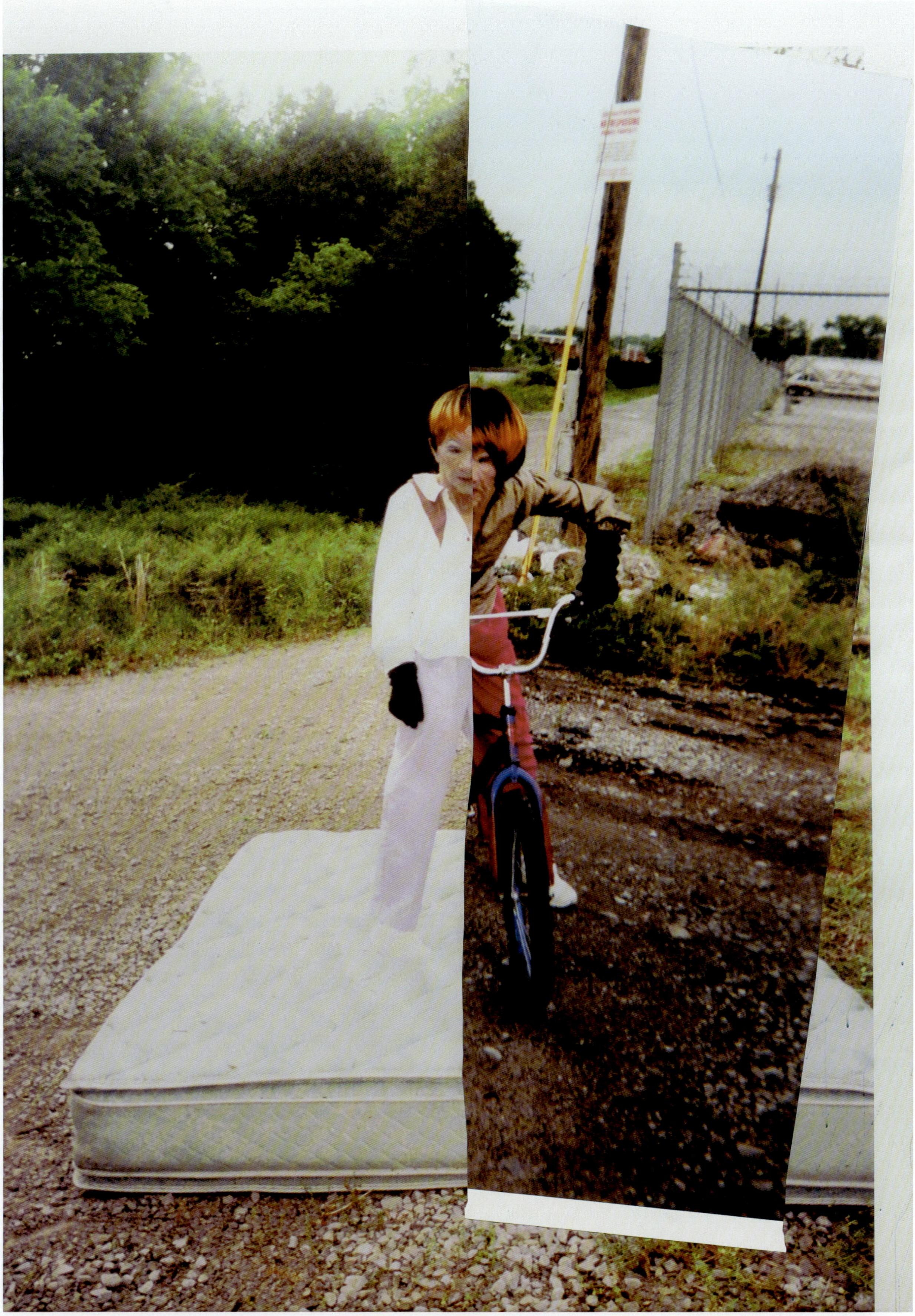

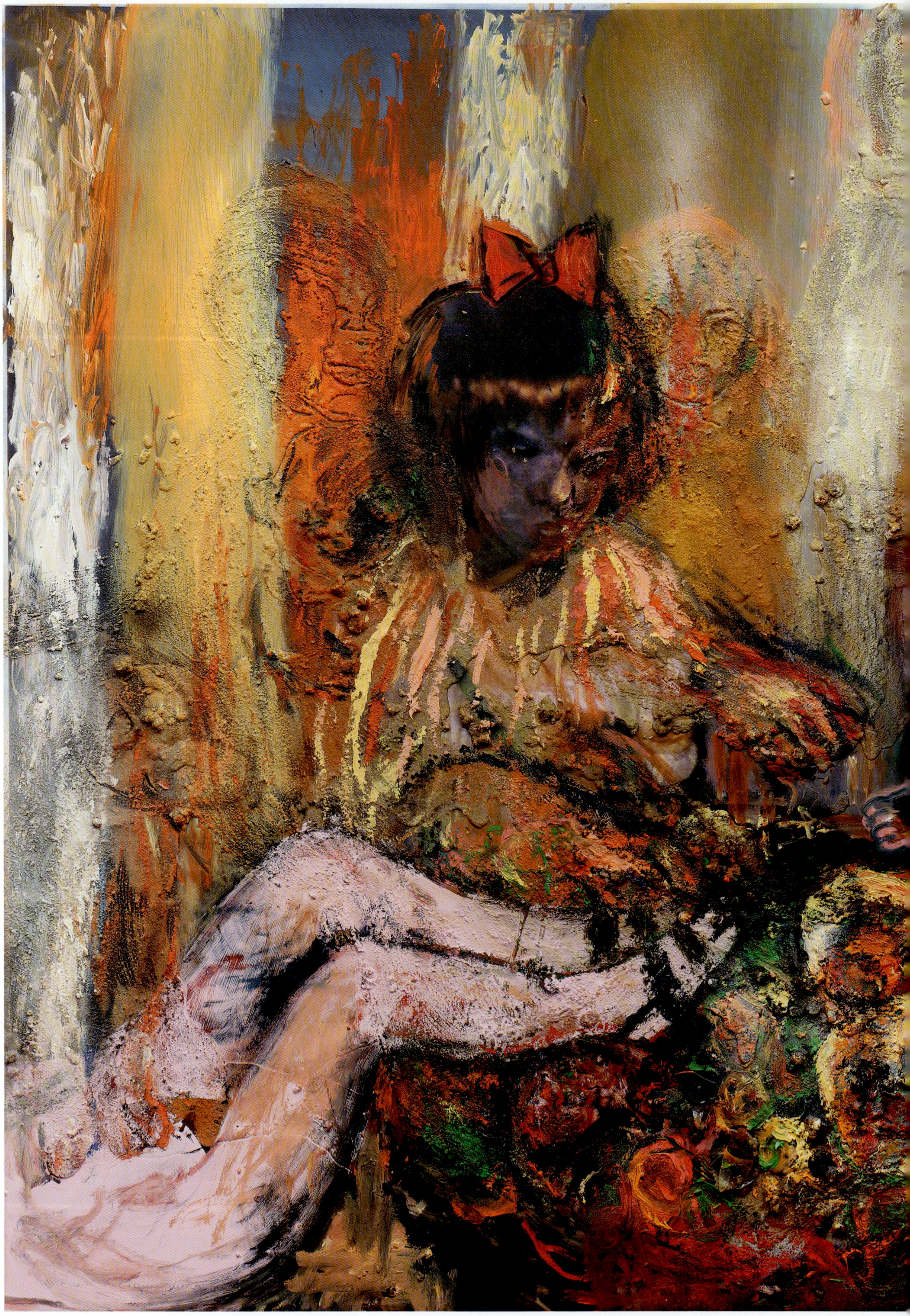

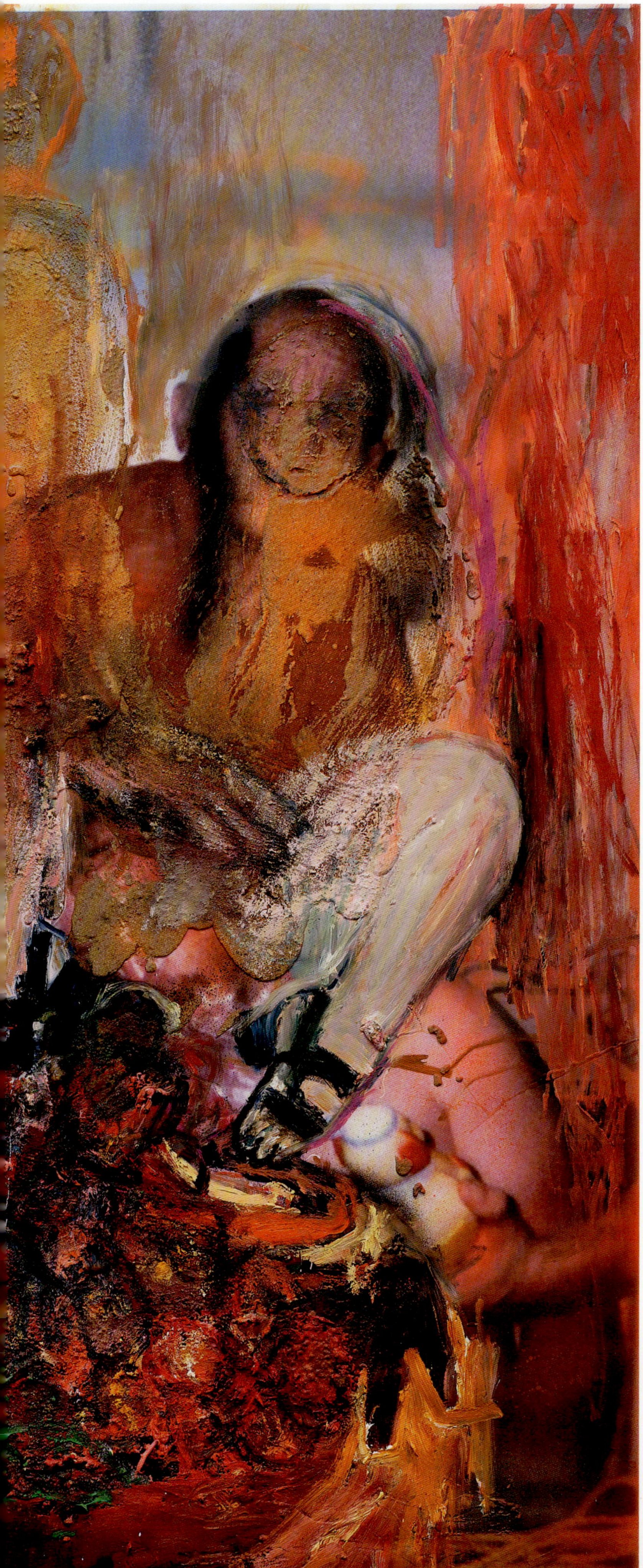

sekret klubs

Richard Flood

Image

The surface of the lake is on fire. It engulfs small islands and leaps across abandoned craft. Debris drifts in sodden tangles while whirlpools swirl into view only to swallow themselves in the flames. Below the burning water, things move with a weedy indolence. Images crawl into focus, linger, and dissolve. Ghostly pictures cohere for a second, but the current pushes them away and another phantasmagoria appears in the rippling liquid. Pushing its way up from the silt and shuddering into place, one image lingers: three girls tremble in placental auras as their spectral and materialized selves merge. These childlike succubi wreathe round a table smothered in a debauch of flowers. Only one of the girls appears to fully inhabit her space, while the others assume a more miasmic presence. There is a kind of slurpy malignancy in the way they've organized themselves, a kind of dissolving fleshiness. These girls are not the mindless, lounging, serpentine houris of Ingres' arrangements. No, the game these children play is filled with intent. The central girl wears a striped pinafore; a big red bow tops her bronze page boy do, and her beautiful, lopsided face is fixed in concentration.

Her pouting mouth indicates seriousness and petulance. She appears to be making an incantatory gesture over the mound of lush, blood-red flowers. These blooms carry the scent of an abattoir mixed with a pollen-dusted country garden. The bouquet is a narcotic trap for strangers adrift on the burning lake.

Hypothesis I

sekret klubs (2010) is painted on a vinyl tarp printed with a photographic enlargement of a still from Harmony Korine's 2009 film *Trash Humpers*. Perhaps because Rita

PRECEDING:
sekret klubs, 2010
Acrylic medium, sand, spray paint, oil, oil stick, popcorn, latex on vinyl
60 x 67½ inches
Courtesy of the Artists and Andrea Rosen Gallery, New York

Ackermann's painting is informed and supported by Korine's film, cinematic allusions appear rife. The drowning woman is a staple in cinema. The actress Shelley Winters was drowned twice, once in *A Place in the Sun* (1951), and, most dramatically, in Charles Laughton's *Night of the Hunter* (1955). In one of the most eerily beautiful sequences in American film, Winters is seen tied into a Model T below the surface of a tranquil lake: tendrils of weeds stir restlessly around the corpse and agitate its flowing hair. The scene is awful but it's also exquisite. Only a year earlier, the Polish actress Bella Darvi played Nefer, "the woman from Babylon," in Michael Curtiz's *The Egyptian*. In the movie's most memorable scene, the hapless hero attempts to drown the copper-wigged Nefer in a lotus pool. Removed from its context, the sequence is a gorgeous one that's more powerful as an abstraction than as a plot twist. Both scenes are inevitably reminiscent of Sir John Everett Millais's juicy painting of *Ophelia* (1852) adrift and akimbo in a drowning stream. With her coppery hair and waterlogged gown filled with a buffet of flowers, Ophelia could almost be the bouquet in Ackermann's painting.

Hypothesis II

Another movie staple is the monstrous child. Below her bangs and downcast gaze, Ackermann's *sekret klubs* girl—one in her legion of girls—could be a contemporary version of the terrifying Rhoda Penmark, the central character in Mervyn LeRoy's *The Bad Seed* (1956) and a postwar symbol of disorder and depravity in the form of a cutie-pie eight-year-old. Rhoda's evil is attributed to her ancestry, which is a convenient device in American culture's inherent anxiety regarding the essentially unknowable nature of children. At the roseate center of *sekret klubs*, there is a similar mystery residing in the closed circle formed by the girls, made even tenser by the spectral faces peering in from below the paint. Another memorable doppelgänger with bangs is the unnamed diminutive nightmare in Federico Fellini's "Toby Dammit" (1968). In this corrosive adaptation of Edgar Allan Poe's short story "Never Bet the Devil Your Head," (1841) the devil is a little girl in a communion dress with moist lips and blood-red fingernails. Her very smile is an invitation—an encouragement—to take command of one's own termination. At the end of the movie, Toby Dammit's severed head, with its look of innocent surprise, might just as well be one of Korine's trash humpers trapped in the pentimento of Ackermann's *sekret klubs*.

Hypothesis III

Of course, Ackermann is, first and foremost, a painter, and it is much more likely that her images come from the long history of painting. Manet and Goya are both very present, with *Luncheon on the Grass* (1862–63) and *Olympia* (1863), respectively, providing the guidelines for the seemingly brilliant carelessness of composition, content, and emotive tension. Nor is Manet's *The Execution of Maximilian* (1868–69) far away, particularly as it leads right back to Goya's *Third of May* (1814) and, through that picture's smoke and screams, into the later "House of the Deaf Man" paintings. It's there, amidst the witches and the warlocks, the shadows and the screams, that *sekret klubs* finds its true heritage as the *klub* turns into a cave and the cave into a curing house for the human condition.

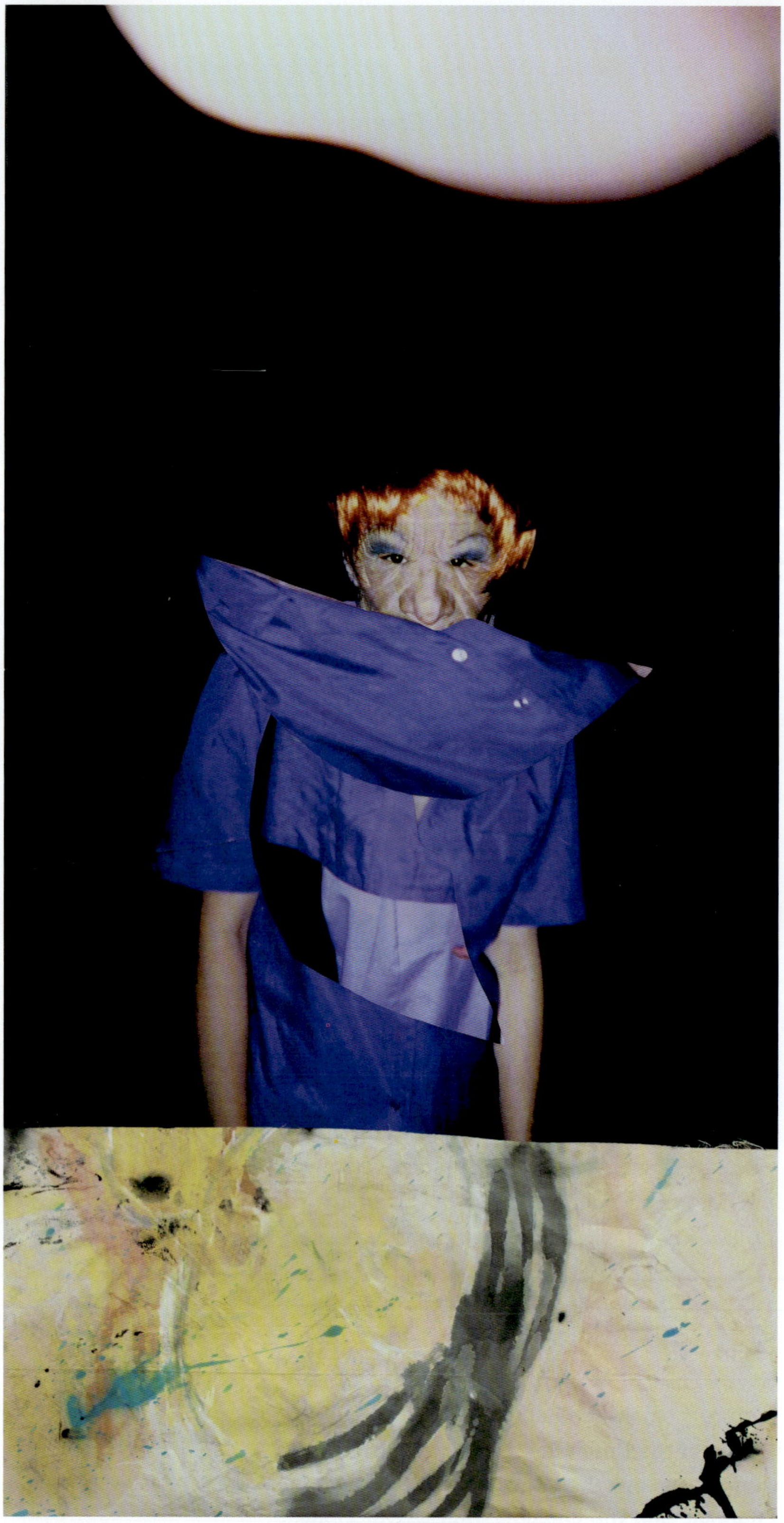

Trouble is Comin, 2010
Acrylic medium on vinyl, enamel
spray paint and ink on canvas
117 x 60 inches
Courtesy of the Artists and
Andrea Rosen Gallery, New York

the last wash, 2010
Acrylic medium, spray paint, enamel, sand, latex, acrylic, oil on vinyl on canvas
87 ¼ x 60 inches
Courtesy of the Artists and Andrea Rosen Gallery, New York

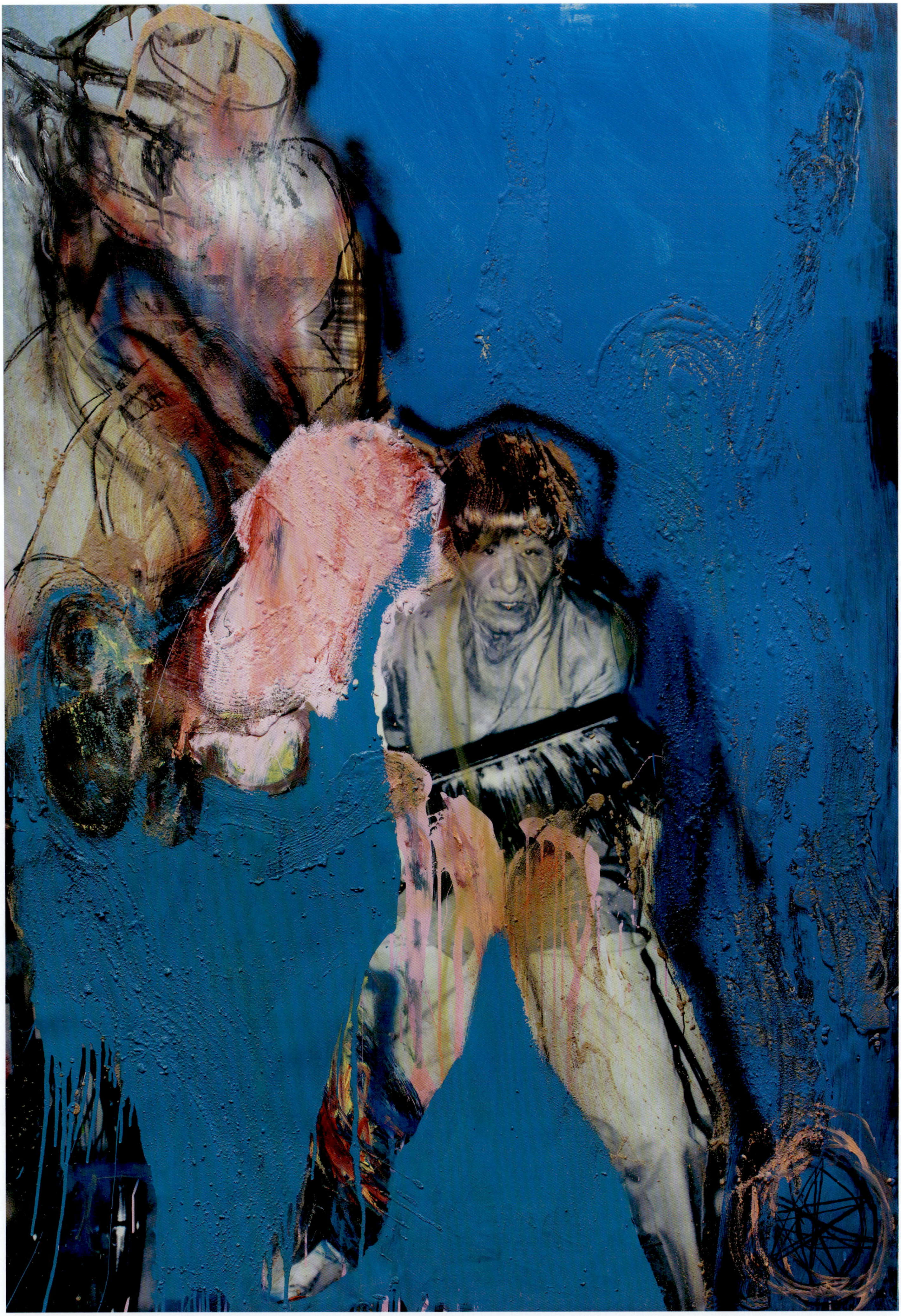

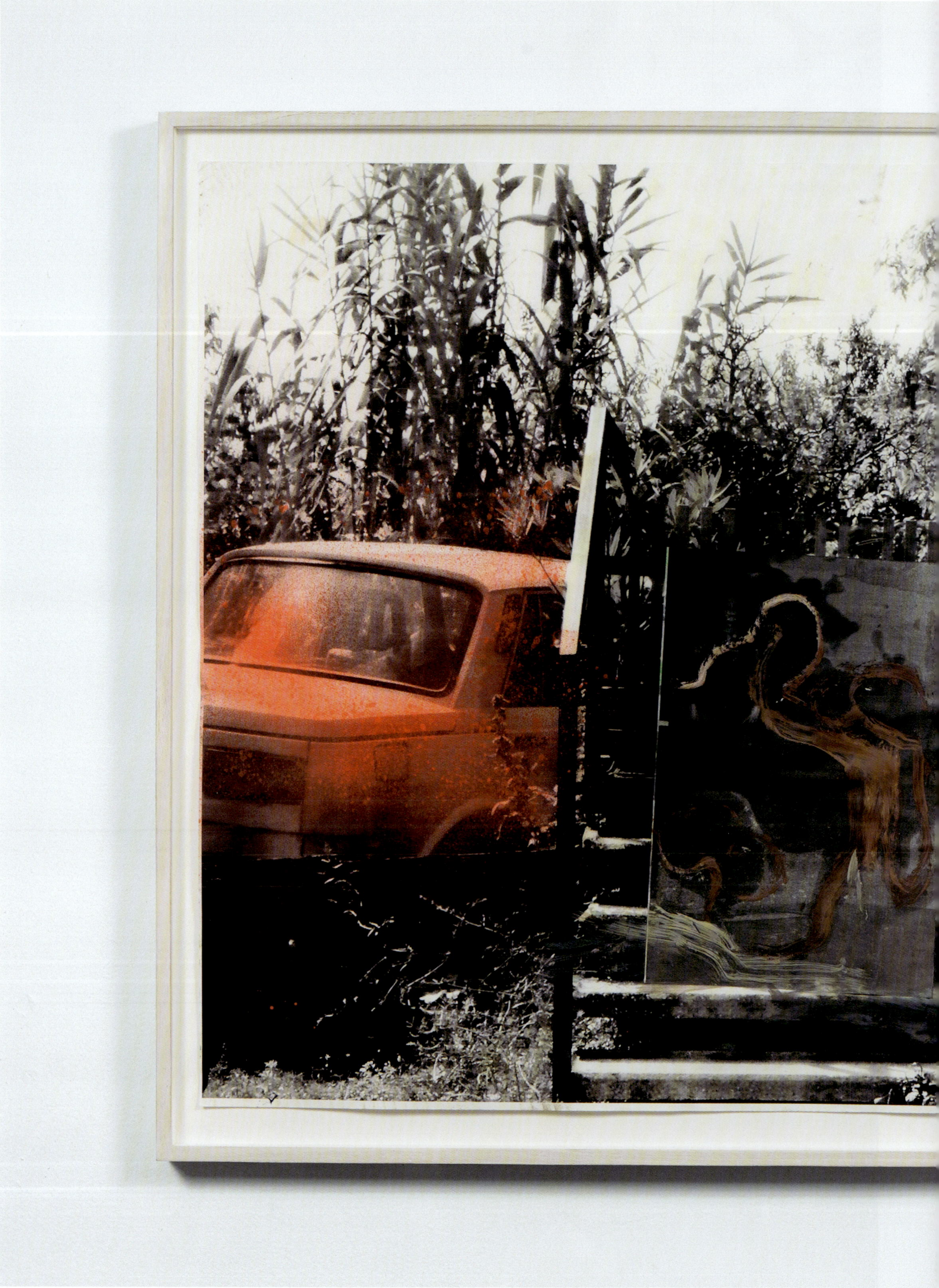

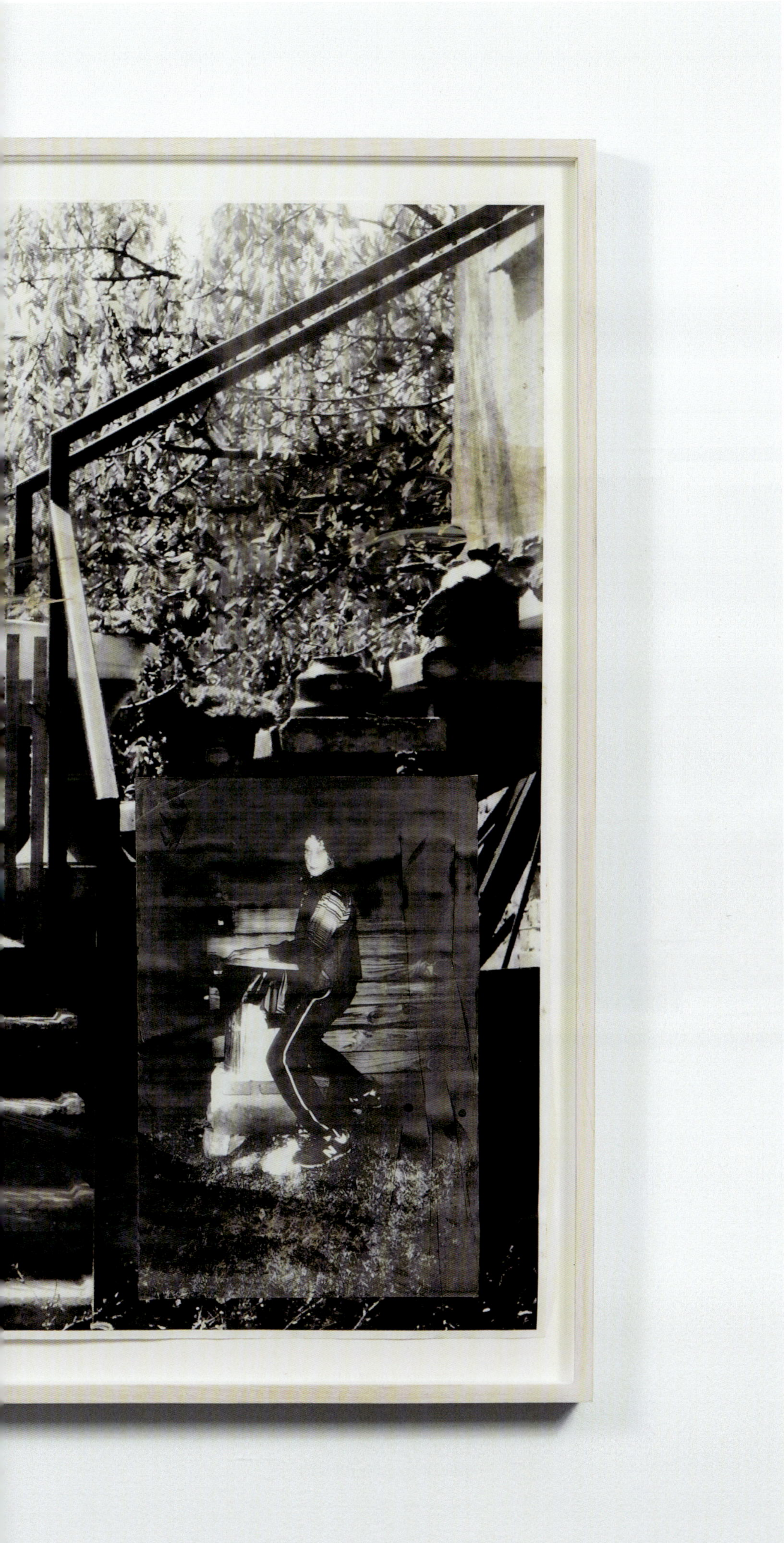

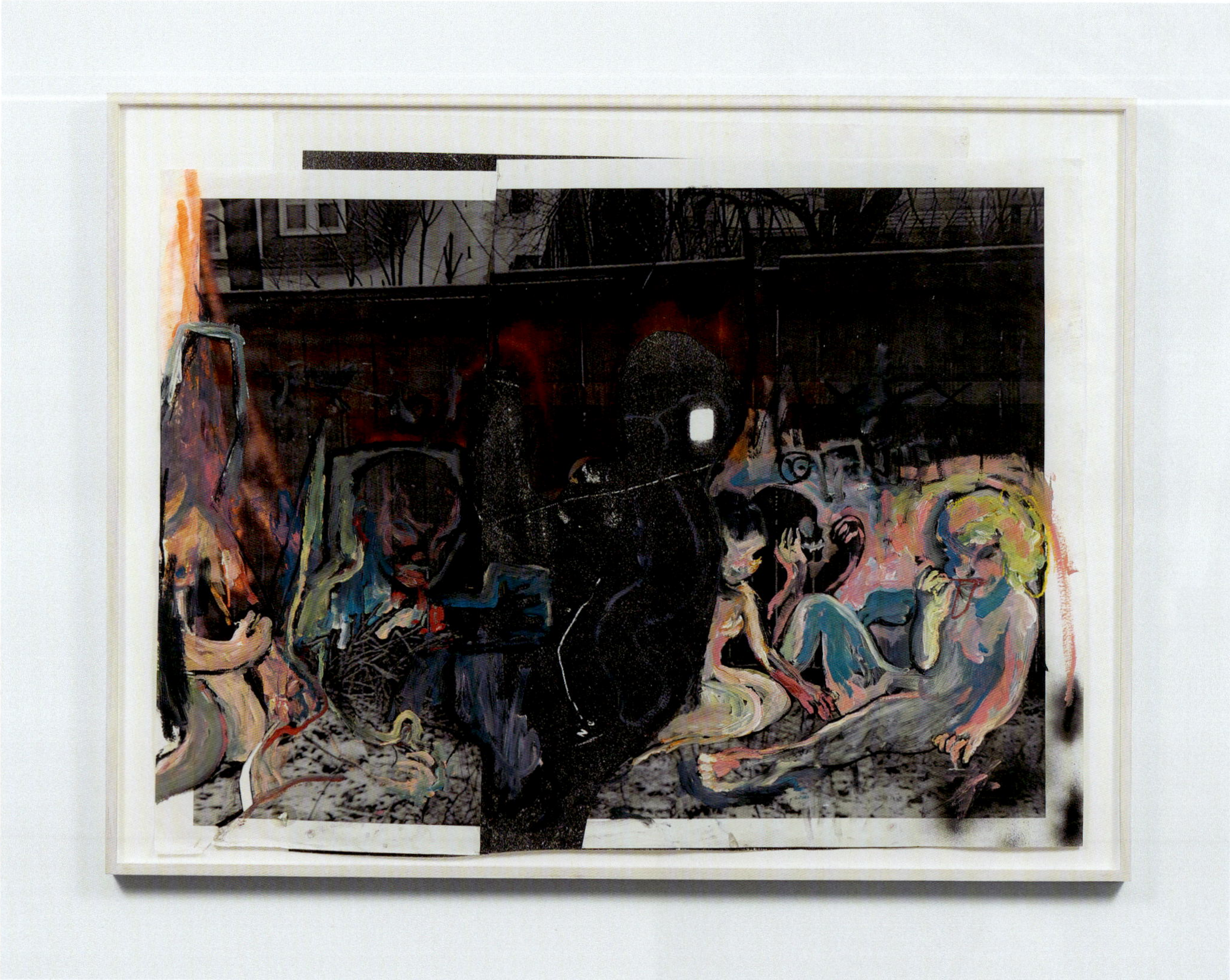

PRECEDING:

of the corn, 2010
Oil, paper cement, spray paint, on printed paper
34 x 45 inches
Courtesy of the Artists and Andrea Rosen Gallery, New York

the one person minaj a trios, 2010
Oil, paper cement, acrylic, charcoal on printed paper
34 x 45 inches
Courtesy of the Artists and Andrea Rosen Gallery, New York

Coming of Age

Piper Marshall

"Erotically charged horror"; "ambivalent arousal"; "playful"; "intimate"; "an orange bonfire erupting in Actionist impasto"; "it's as if Hans Bellmer used geometric lines to break open a vortex"; "fast and slow"; "thick and thin." Criticism is adulterated when seasoned with such pseudo references; the artists are likened to the artist's artist of the moment, while their works are embellished with literary devices: simile and hyperbole or alliteration and allusion. These cool and slick descriptive tendencies, once applied, slip over the artwork as a thick coat of shiny lacquer—a social lubricant, if you will. They are as critically nutritious as the Zagat guide descriptions they resemble (if we were to forgo the meal itself). The borderline arguments follow the same formula: appreciation garnished with a dash of outsider art. They are delivered with an invocation of mythology, followed by some phantasmagoric description. The rhetoric is geared toward artistic multiplicity, or an appreciation for the abject. The effect is full—or perhaps well credentialed—yet never fleshed out. Why the lip service?

The most common arguments brought to bear when describing the work before us invoke the psychosexual cast of characters set forth by Henry Darger and Hans Bellmer. These artists are interchangeable with the Norseman or the Brothers Grimm. The justification for this friendly reading dives into questions of both style and social etiquette. The politically correct manner of writing, in this case, establishes a non–art historical trajectory. Behind the profane and avant-garde, we are asked once again to discover our own polite "interrogations" of culture. These celebrated masters are those whom the gothic *jeunes filles* service. While the former are canonized as the kings of outsider art, the fate of their lesser halves, the teen princesses, remains opaque.

The narrative arc of a girl's journey into womanhood revolves around virginity, loss, and the eventual lesson learned. These allegories are necessarily moralist on one hand and gendered on the other. When applied to the Rita Ackermann and Harmony Korine collage *one person minaj a trios* (2010), the trope is stalled. In the center of the composition a congregation of bald, cat-eyed tweens beats off amongst ghostly figures, the youths rendered with oil stick and paper cement on printed paper. No virtue is lost in self-fulfillment. The equivocation of the protagonists is palpable, caught as they are on the cusp of pleasure.

Suspending a discussion of the dynamism of the artwork, this transgressive collage is an invitation to edify ourselves with the well-worn theories of feminist film critic Laura Mulvey, who champions film with deconstructive narrative in "Visual Pleasure and Narrative Cinema" (1973/75). According to Mulvey, in (a vilified) traditional cinema, the woman's character is relegated to the position of scenery against which the action unfolds. One could argue that the artwork presented by Ackermann and Korine disrupts hierarchy and a larger order via its many cuts, layers, and collaged elements. However, the critical writing that attempts to understand and prescribe this dynamism follows a structure that imposes itself on the work. The figures, and their forebears, are then tamed.

And why is there no recourse? A deeper look at the structure of the artwork is necessary. The collage is comprised of Korine's film stills printed on paper, then layered and spliced together, and on top of which Ackermann draws. The opposing mediums —photography, collage, oil stick—are pasted together. Each strategy comes with historical references: postmodern photography or the neo-expressionism of the 1980s. This pairing of opposites renders the collaged photographs an unstable ground on which to draw. In splicing together the two strategies, no clear statement is made. It is the unyielding, schizophrenic composition that makes these characters would-be horror-filled fetish objects, dynamic in their opposition, yet vulnerable because of it.

Stuck in its conflation, the critical machine never quite turns over. The chain of references, allusions, and tropes gives a frisson of pleasure in recognition, but this infinite regression is in opposition to the experience of the work itself, whose rough energy and ambiguity—in effect, the work's own matrix of pleasure and suspension—is not without a high school–notebook aesthetic, all the more tenderly charming in that it allows us to "place" and domesticate it through vocabulary—rather like after school detention.

Soundtrack to Chlorine, 2010
Acrylic, oil, charcoal, spray paint, paper cement, tempera, printed paper on printed paper
34 x 45 inches
Courtesy of the Artists and Andrea Rosen Gallery, New York

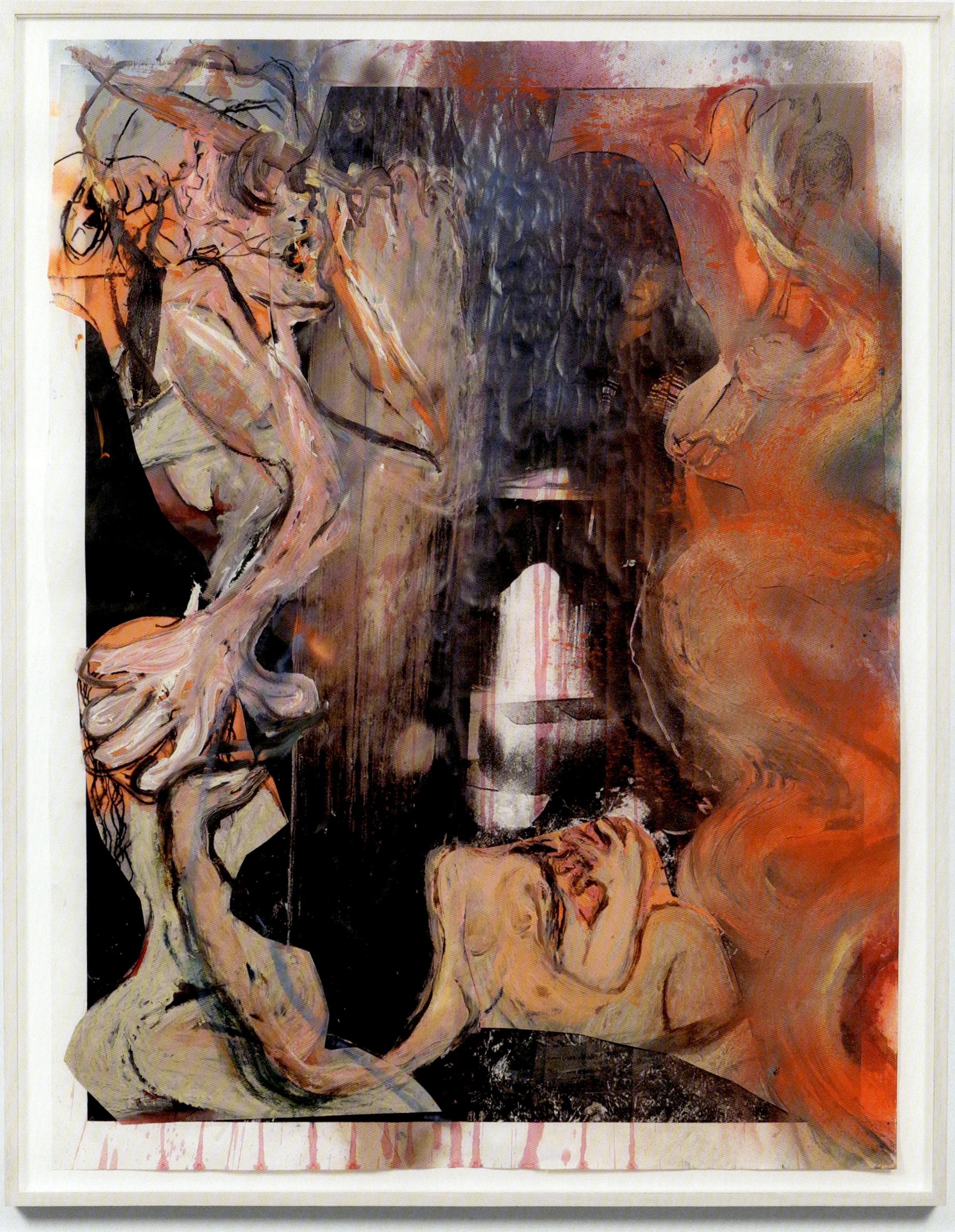

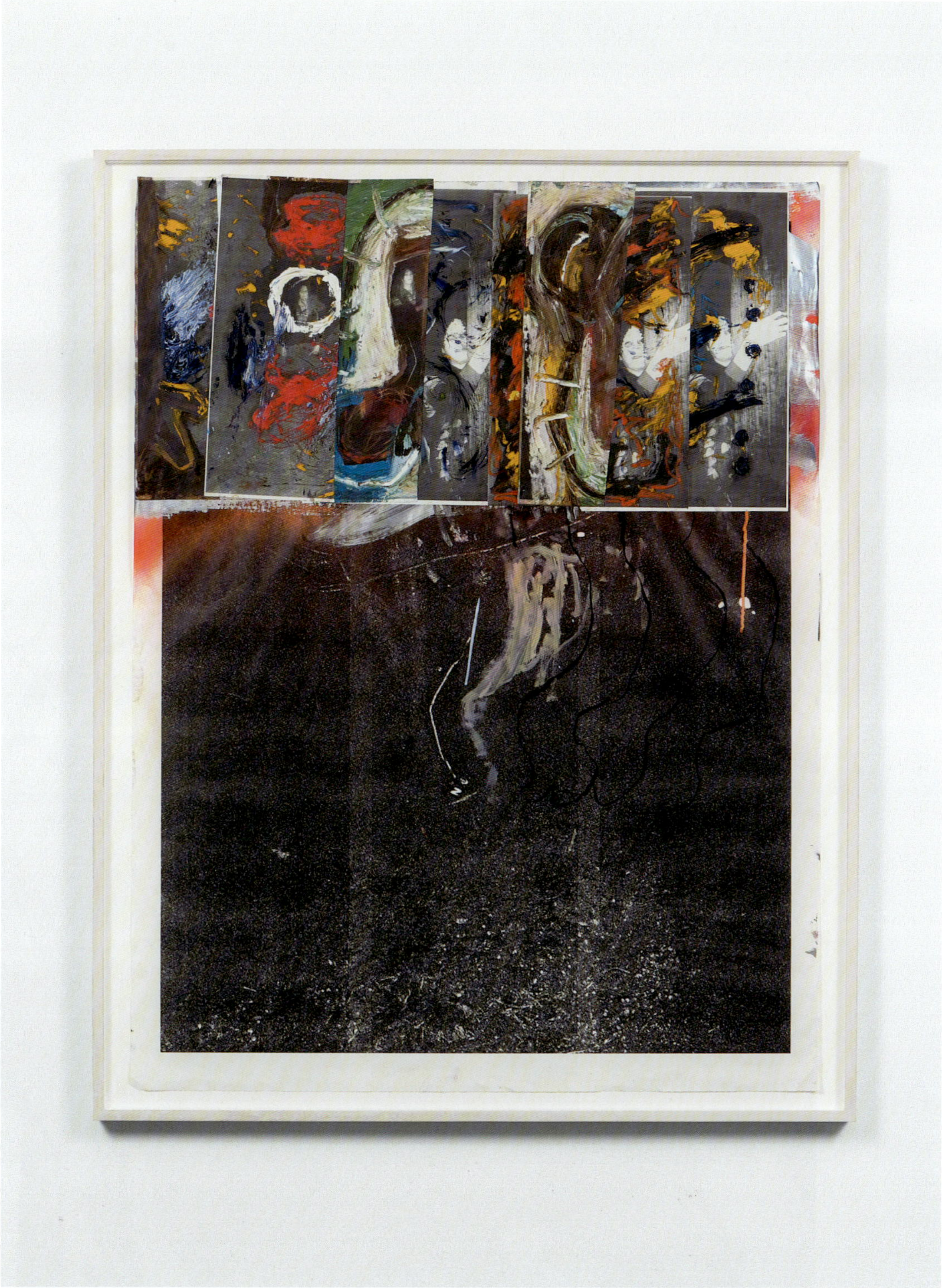

sorry i was scorned this way, 2010
Oil, paper cement, spray paint, charcoal, acrylic, tempera, printed paper on printed paper
34 x 45 inches
Courtesy of the Artists and Andrea Rosen Gallery, New York

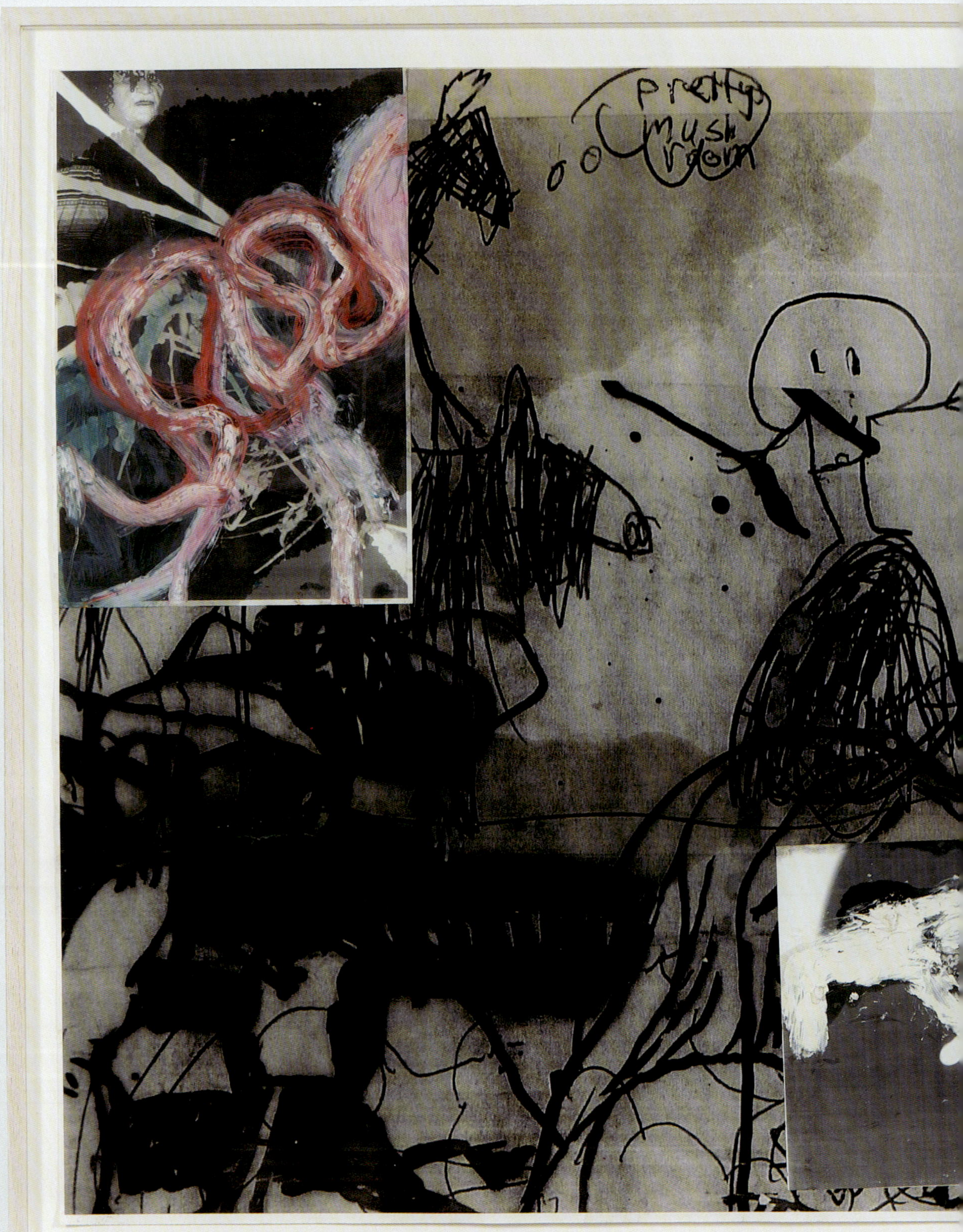
pretty
mush
room

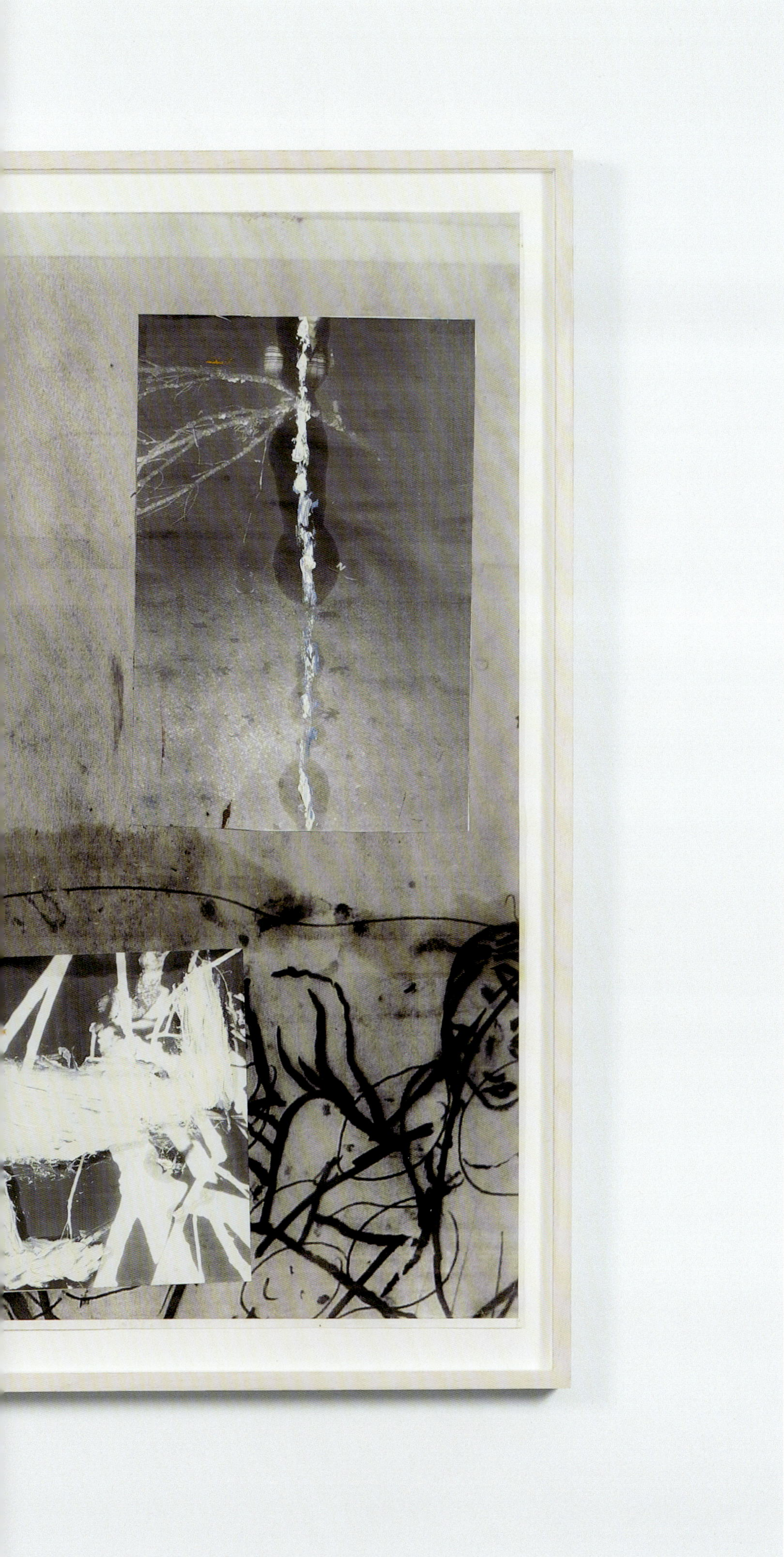

What did the drawing say to the movie still?

Antoine Catala

In "Shadow Fux," the photos are movie stills. Not video frames, but photographic stills taken by Harmony Korine around the movie set for *Trash Humpers* (2009). The photographs document the film (they were taken in part for that purpose) and, as exhibited side by side—or, one could say, frame by frame—each carries a narrative element.

These *Trash Humpers* stills are the raw material of the exhibition, the primary matter for Rita Ackermann's intervention.

The two photographs that comprise the backdrop of *frail tech* (2010) and *it's showtime cloaks* (2010) depict the same space as the backdrop of the film: everyday derelict Nashville suburbia. These photos, unlike others on display in the show, do not feature any of the movie's protagonists—no trash humpers here. Yet because of the nature of the still, and within the context of "Shadow Fux," humpers are lurking around.

So, in that context, what can a drawing say to a movie still?

(1+1)?

In *frail tech* (2010), a crop of a graffitied wall features at its center a mushroom stick figure holding a gun and dressed in a skirt. The mushroom guy seems to be graffitied directly onto the wall as photographed by

PRECEDING:
frail tech, 2010
Oil, paper cement, printed paper
on printed paper
34 x 45 inches
Courtesy of the Artists and
Andrea Rosen Gallery, New York

Korine. Or is it? Other components in the work indicate differently: multiple small photographs are collaged atop the original background and are further drawn on; each addition could be interpreted uniquely (a squiggle, a lightning bolt, a trail of urine). At the bottom right-hand corner is one of Ackermann's sexual nymphets. The additive complements are seamlessly merged with the background.

The drawing enters the photographic image from within and alters it at its core. There is a confusing homogeneity (for the viewer) in the plasticity of the work; it is hard to distinguish between the eye of the photographer and the hand of the draftswoman, or vice versa.

What else can a drawing say to a movie still?

(1-1)?

In *it's showtime cloaks,* the process is quasi-reversed. The drawing overrides the totality of the background photograph; it covers all but a small part of it, creating a small window through which we may enter.

The window plays a double role here, for it acts on two different planes. On the drawing plane (where the drawing resides), it is read as a shadow, a ghostly figure, a negative space. It was there at some point—or so it seems—but got carved away. Looking inside the window, we enter another plane and see the streets of Nashville where the project started—or rather a mere glimpse of it: the hood of a car, some treetops, a front wheel. The fact of the matter is, photographs are incredibly resilient. From just a glance at this fragment, one can picture the entire scene: the cars, the street, a casual passerby, trash humpers and their little corner of Nashville, the suburban forest nearby.

One could imagine the moments just before the photo was taken and the moments right after: the heat, the smell of the street, and the sound of the city. That's because we are dealing with a movie still, a photograph that carries a strong narrative within.

The drawing acts as a frame, surrounds the photograph, literally, and informs it. It's a complement, a vortex. It activates it by covering it, but paradoxically, in no way obfuscates it; the photo and what it represents remain intact. The two planes coexist, but at different levels; they act as reliefs for each other, but they do not share a common language. In *it's showtime cloaks,* the drawing didn't say much to the photograph. These moments, when there is a failure to interact, are actually the most valuable parts of the collaborative project.

So, what did
the drawing say to
the movie still?

+ or -?

The drawings are stored onto the photograph, which itself has its own archival purpose. The archival process is accumulative in nature; it occurs like sedimentation does, layer upon layer, the movie still acting as the bottom stratum. The result reads like a geological map, unveiling the properties of each individual stratum. Ackermann and Korine's interventions share a common ground—the same surface—but each body of work is stored on different strata and is made out of different matter. The way we see images is hardwired into the brain, but there's one connection for movie stills and another for drawings. Movie stills embody a real thing;[1] drawings are communions.

---

[1] "Film is a real thing and as a real thing it is not imitation. It does not reflect on life, it embodies the life of the mind." –Ernie Gehr

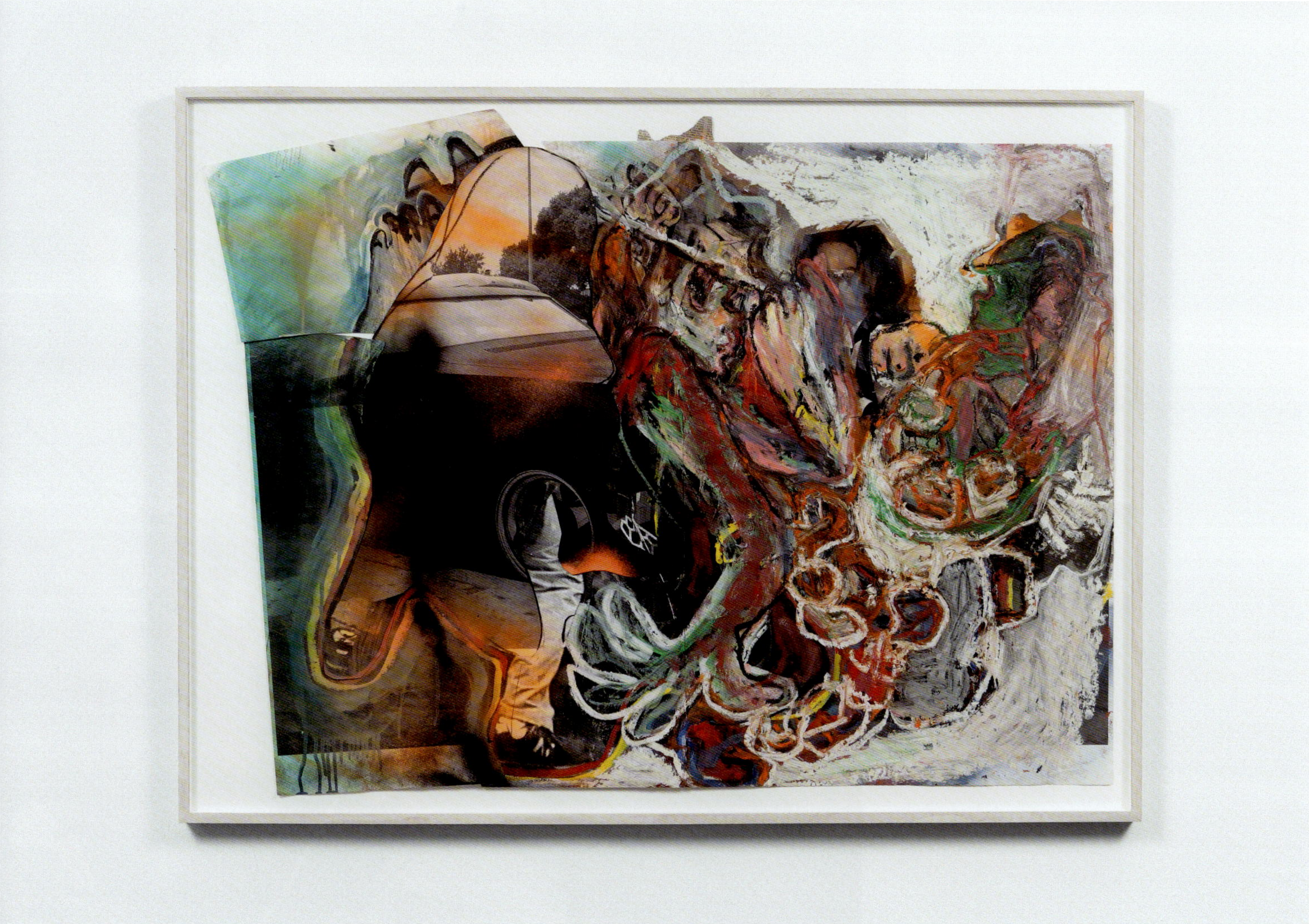

<u>it's showtime cloaks</u>, 2010
Acrylic, oil, charcoal, spray paint,
paper cement, printed paper
on printed paper
34 x 45 inches
Courtesy of the Artists and
Andrea Rosen Gallery, New York

FOLLOWING:
<u>me versus the light</u>, 2010
Oil, paper cement, charcoal,
orange peel, staples, cigarettes,
permanent marker, printed
paper on printed paper
34 x 45 inches
Private Collection, New York

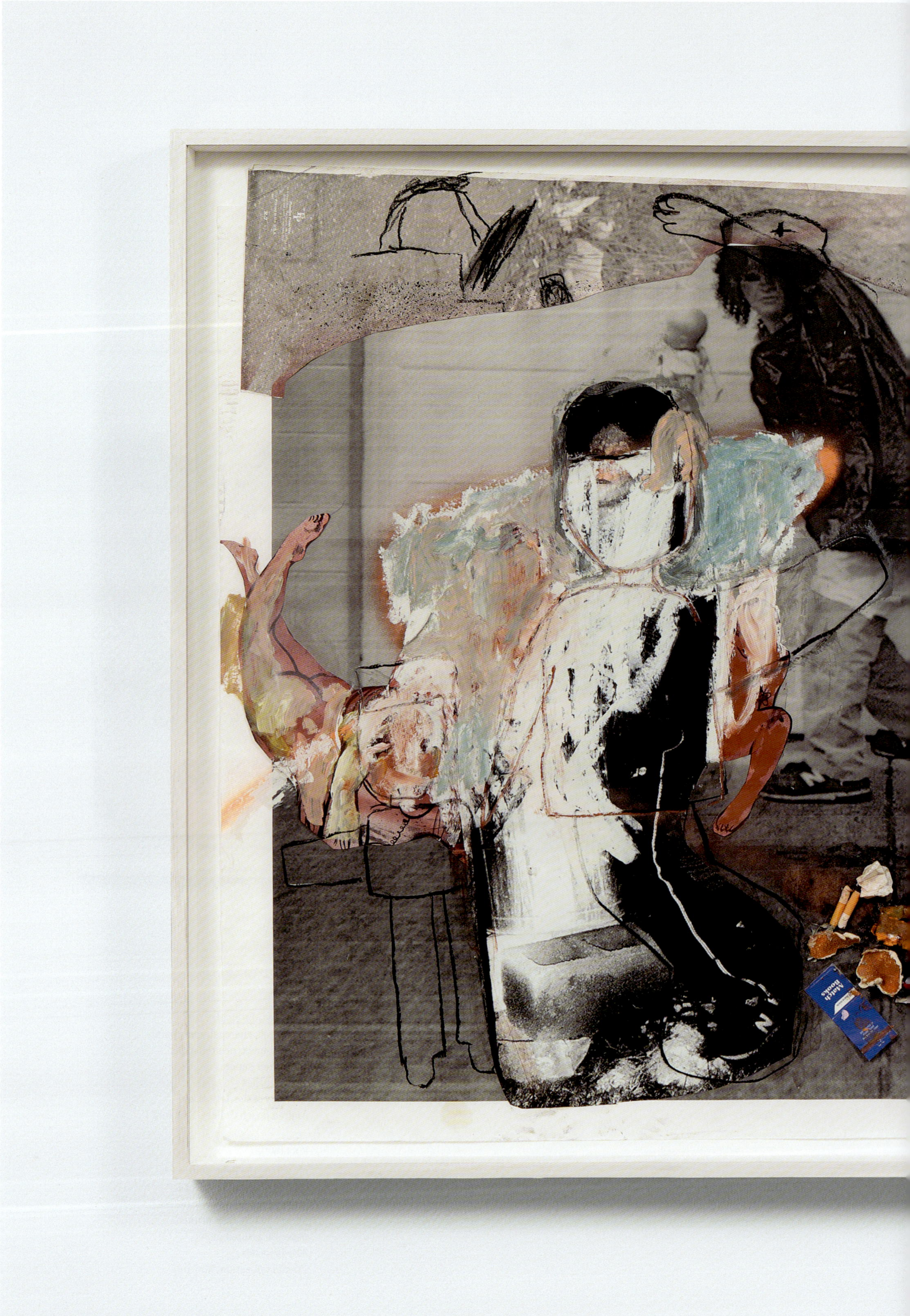

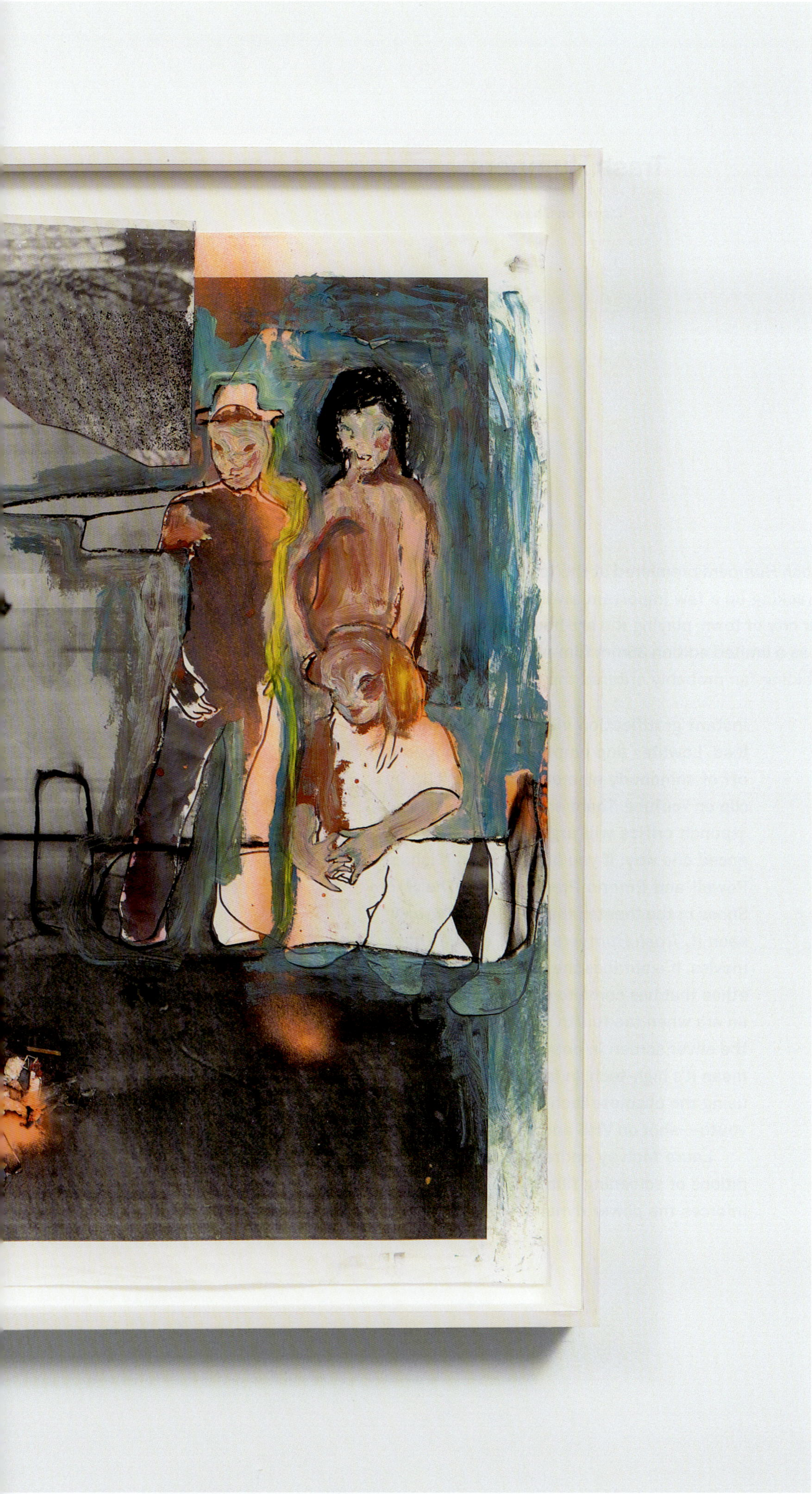

Trash Humpers

Cameron Shaw

Harmony Korine's *Trash Humpers* premiered at the Toronto International Film Festival in 2009. It ran the festival circuit, racking up a few important awards and even more disgusted walkouts. It may have traveled to your city or town, playing the art-house theater or local café. For the rich and highbrow, it was offered as a limited edition 35mm film print or VHS tape in an auteur-customized case. Your modest, law-abiding fan probably ordered the DVD—patiently awaiting the mail—or bought instant gratification via the official download. Lowlifes and empty-pockets ripped it off of somebody else or watched it clip by clip on YouTube. There are some movies that staunch critics will argue must be experienced one way: if you haven't seen Michael Powell and Emeric Pressburger's *The Red Shoes* in the theater, then you haven't really seen it. *Trash Humpers* is not one of those movies. It embraces the catch-as-catch-can ethos that has come to define viewership in an era when the fourth screen has eclipsed the silver screen in popularity. That doesn't mean it's high-tech. In fact, it was produced using the obsolete technologies of Korine's youth—shot on VHS and edited on VCRs.

Laura Mulvey addressed how the conditions of screening films in the theater reinforces the power dynamics of the cinema in her classic psychoanalytic treatise "Visual Pleasure and Narrative Cinema." Writing in 1973—the year Harmony Korine was born—she couldn't have predicted the ways in which reality TV and the Internet would further transform the scopophilic instinct. Defying traditional narrative cinema, *Trash Humpers* has the rambling logic and unfeigned intimacy of a family home video (if your clan consisted of deranged geriatric vampires who fake-fuck trash). The improvisation is so convincing in part because the family is Korine's. The director stars alongside his wife Rachel and two friends. Wearing masks visually located somewhere between old people and burn victims, the team terrorizes the streets of his hometown with grunts, screeches, and song.

Watch or read any interview with Korine and by its end you'll have gleaned he's as interested in making films as he is creating myths. A storyteller, fabulist, and white griot, he once told me *Trash Humpers* was based on a crew of elderly folks at a makeshift nursing home near the house where he grew up in Nashville. He would see the Peeping Toms spying into his pretty neighbor's window late at night. They wore white nursing shoes and black turtlenecks. They only listened to Herman's Hermits. Korine has repeated this story over and over again always focusing on a different set of haunting details. Whether this sinister group ever existed only he really knows—or maybe he doesn't. The memories of the younger mind are plagued with anxieties. We remember things that never were, because they speak to where we are now.

That is ultimately where the power of *Trash Humpers* lies—in the way it speaks to how we watch, consume and live now. In its last fifteen minutes—after an hour of virtually unexplained mayhem and murder—one of Korine's inventions delivers what some might call the message of the film: "This is important," he stammers from behind Coke-bottle glasses and a ridiculous bobbed wig. "You don't really understand the importance, but sometimes when I drive through these streets at night, I can smell the pain of all these people living in here. I can smell how all these people are just trapped in their lives—their day-to-day lives." It's a monologue about freedom and subversion, the dangers of conformity and the restorative power of anarchy. It is understood by that point that after our current conventions of success and stability die out, these characters will still be around to advocate for a new destruction, leading what they call the "balanced life." They'll live this way forever.

It is this balance—this creative reversal—that's contained in the collaboration between Harmony Korine and Rita Ackermann. Working back and forth, but never in the same place, the artists took stills from the movie and printed them on vinyl—just as films in the theater have long been projected onto vinyl screens. The images were cut up, collaged with canvas, and painted upon. Here the two artists become one. The history of painting and filmmaking collide. The figurative dissolves into the abstract. In one work, a character's arm morphs into nothing more than watery brushstrokes. Action becomes everlasting energy.

Deleted scenes from the film
Trash Humpers (2009)
Director, writer Harmony Korine;
Editing Leo Scott; Starring Paul
Booker, Dave Cloud, and Chris
Crofton, et al; Produced by
Alcove Entertainment, agnès b.

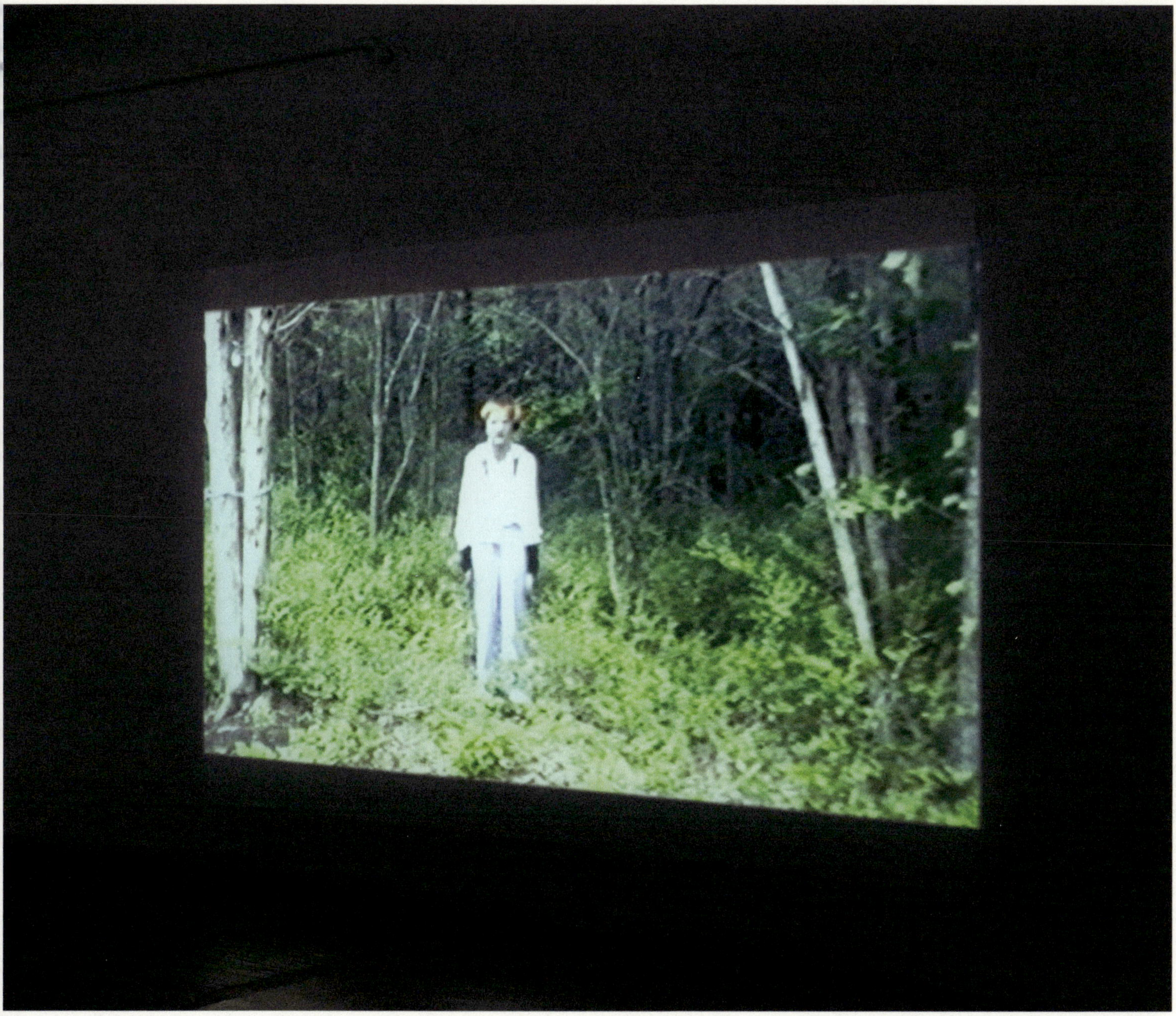

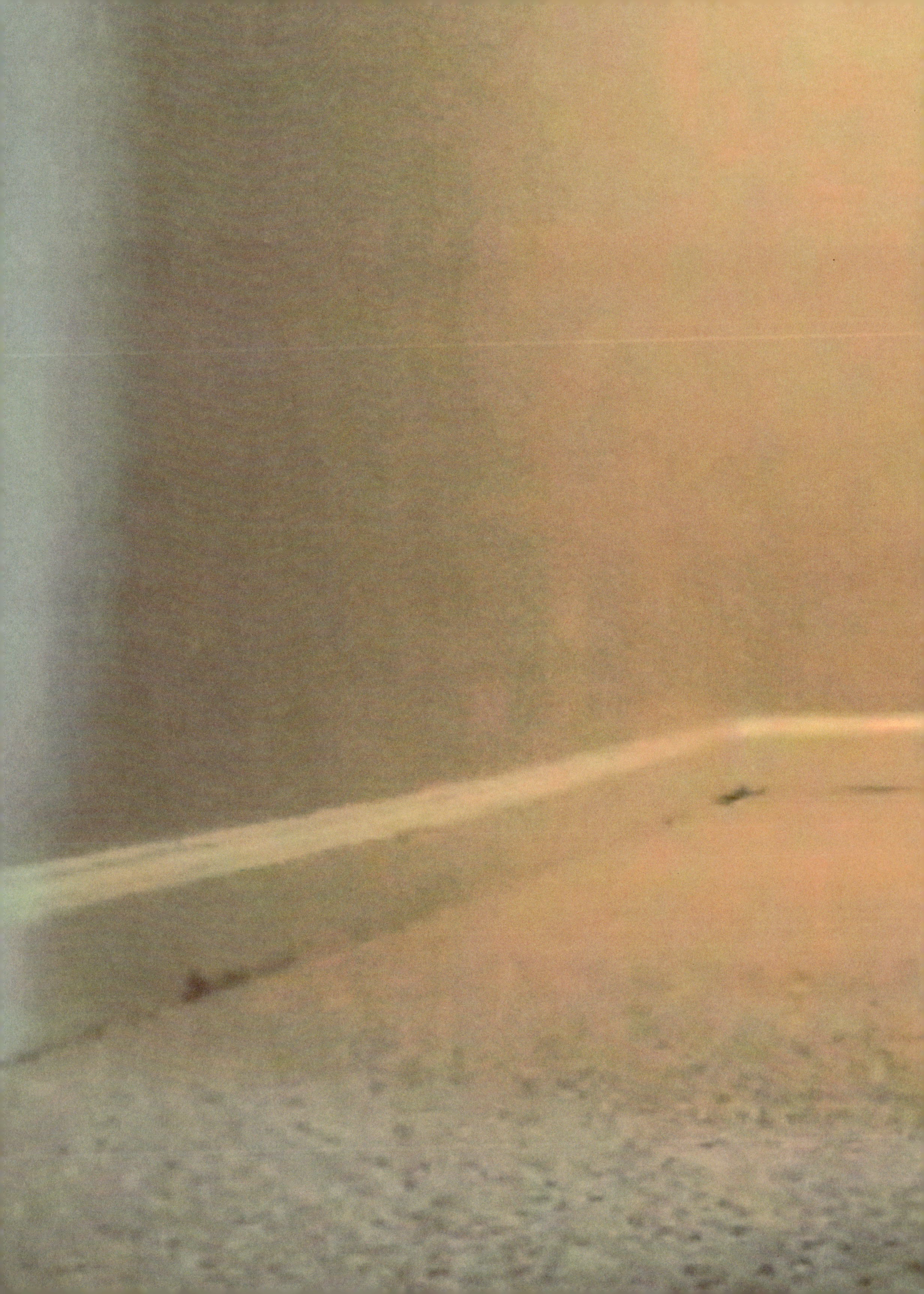

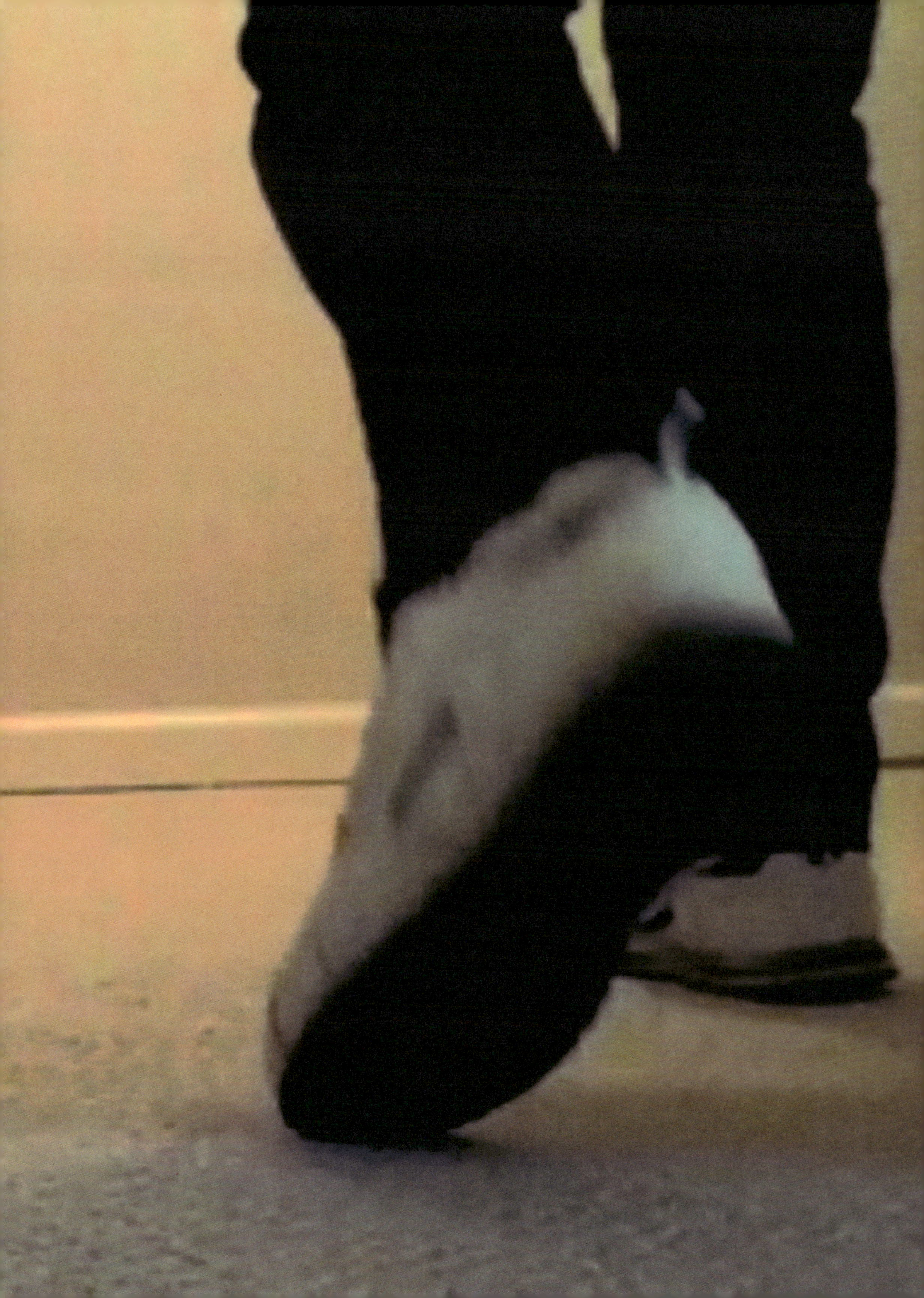

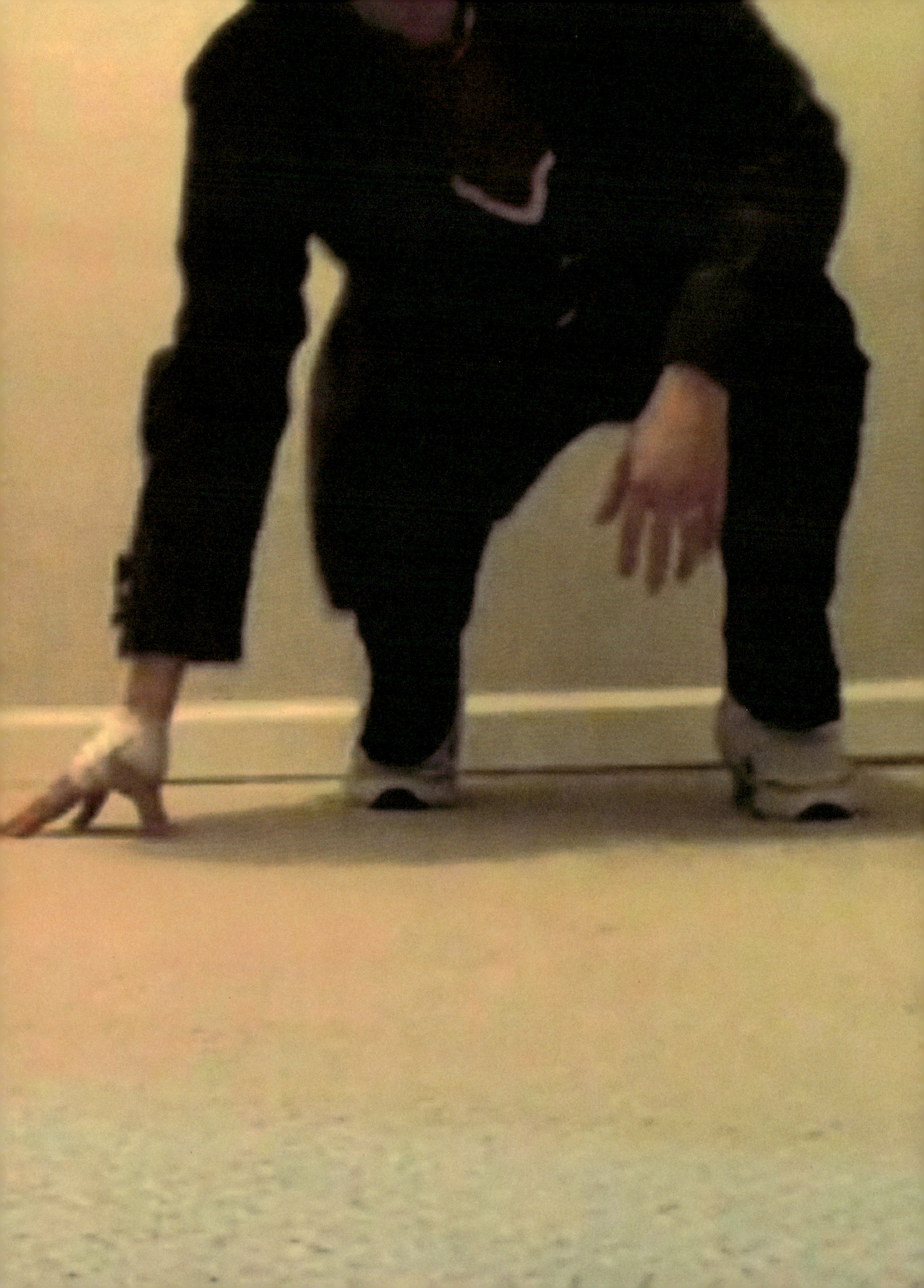

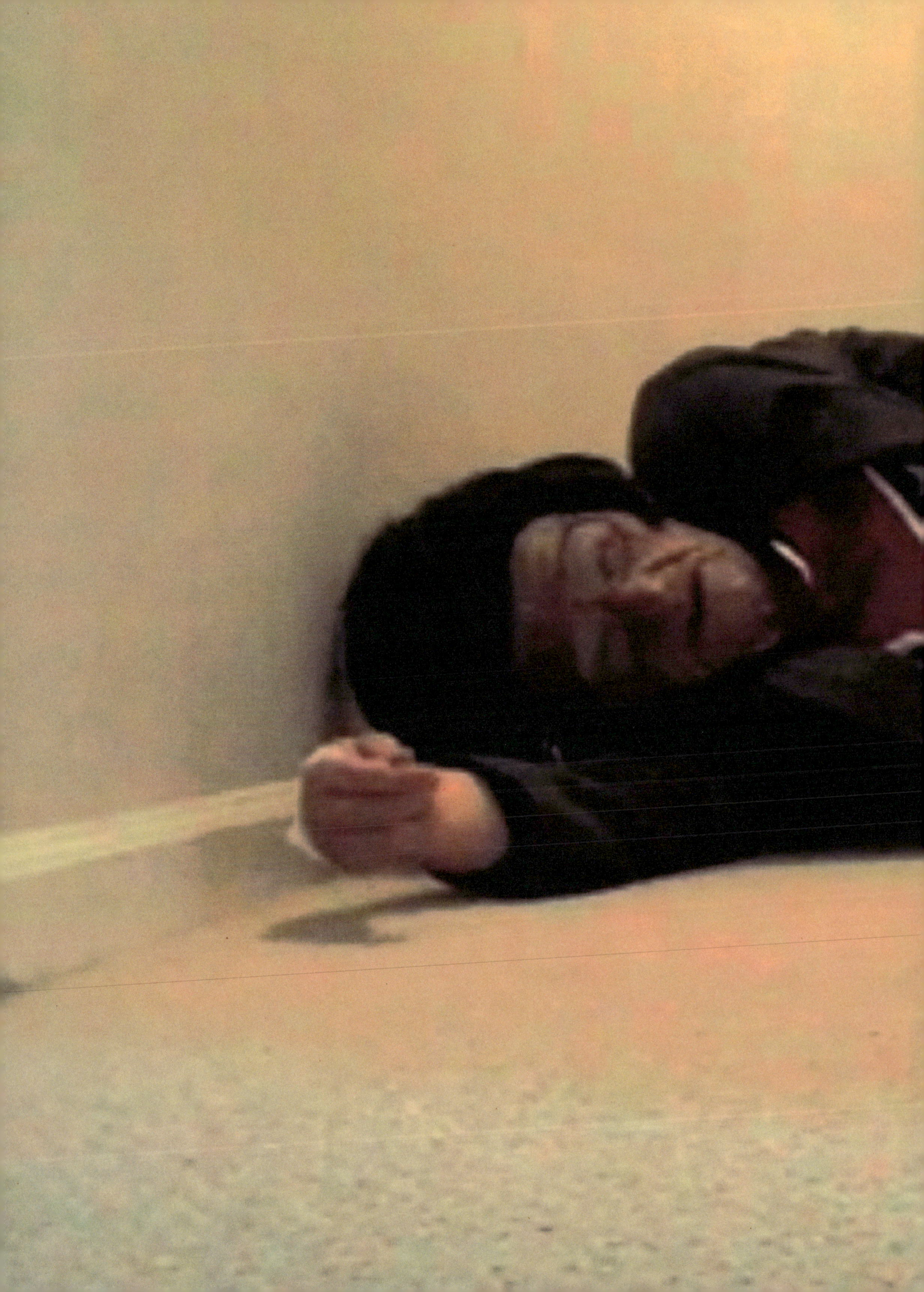

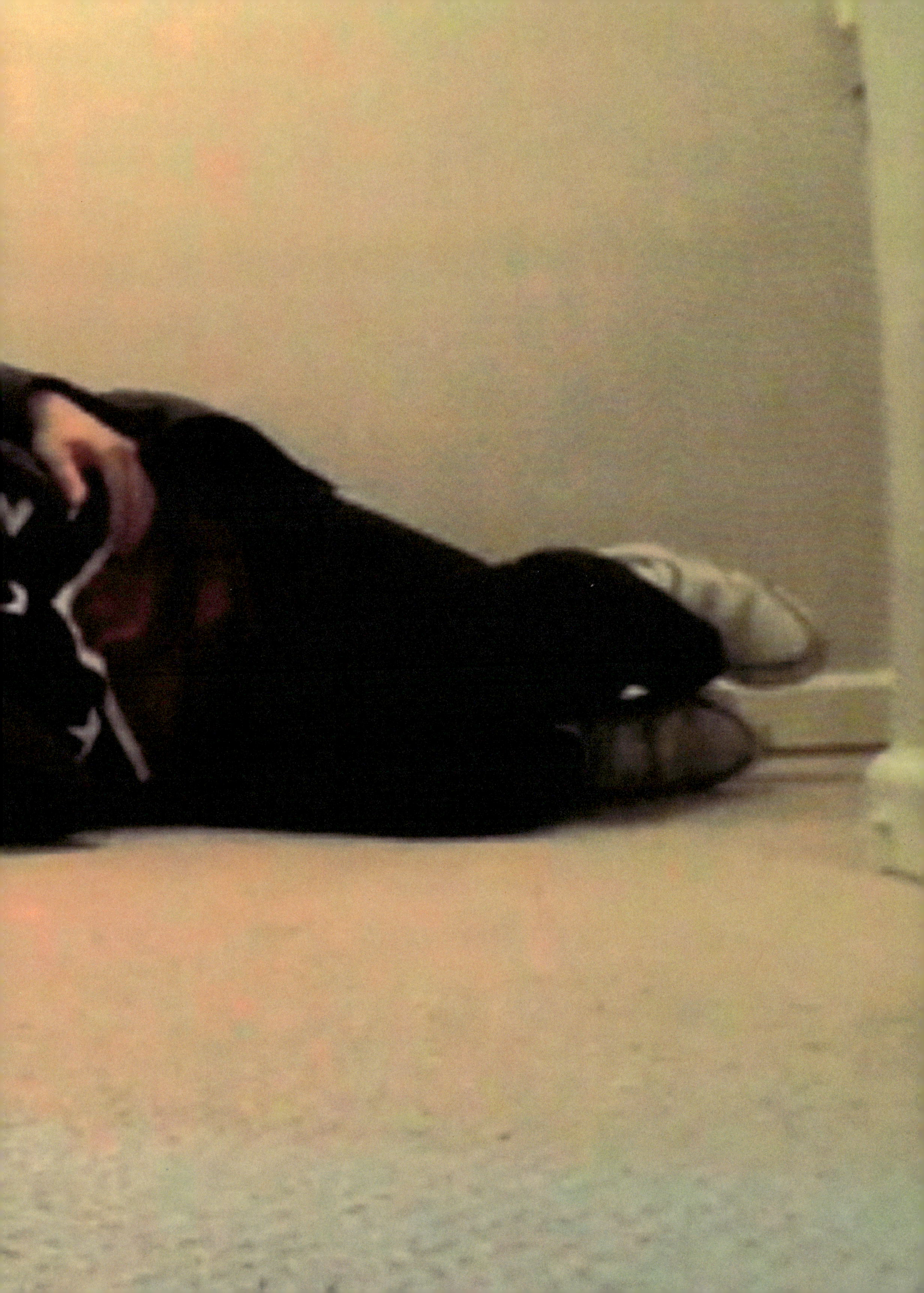

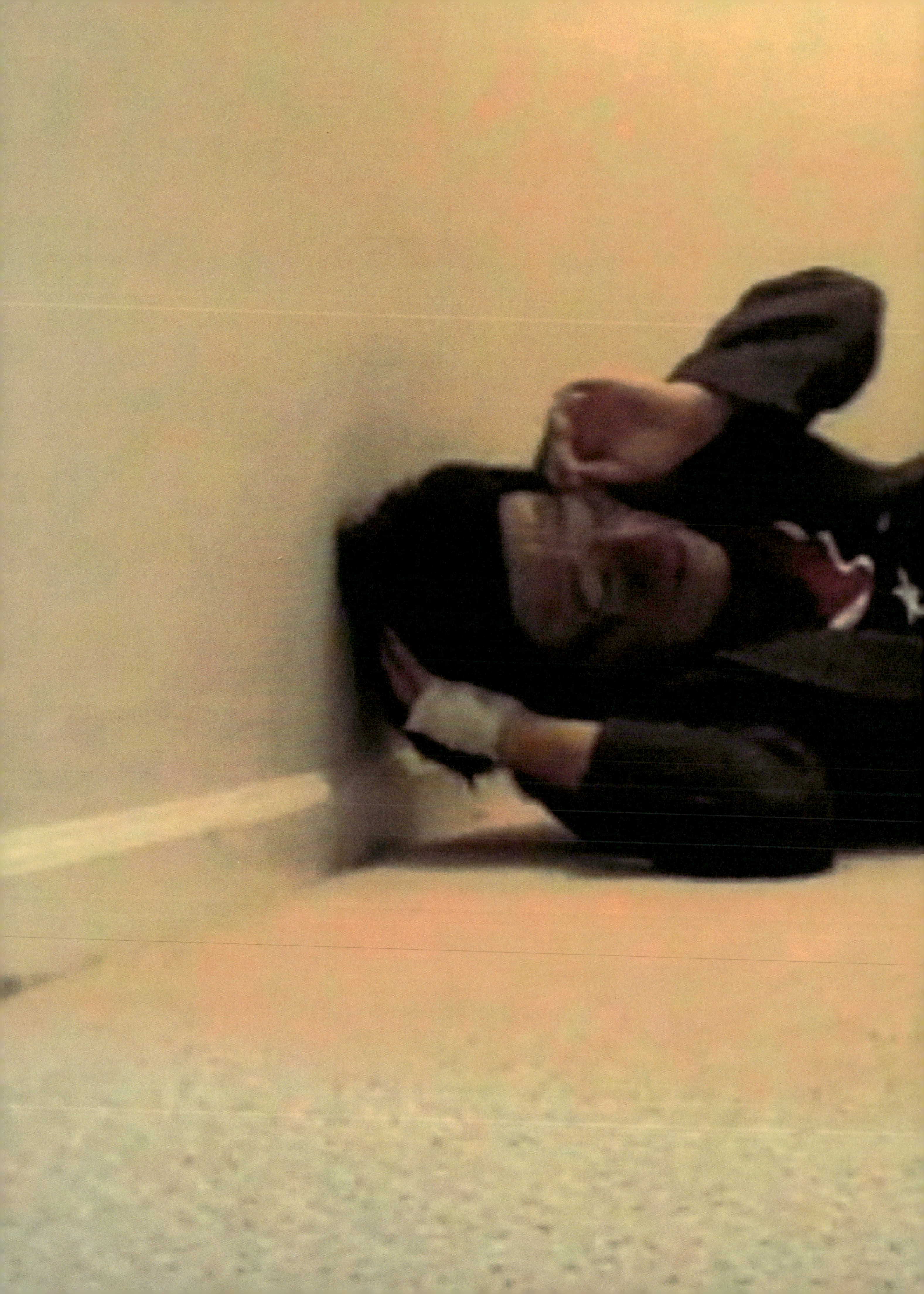

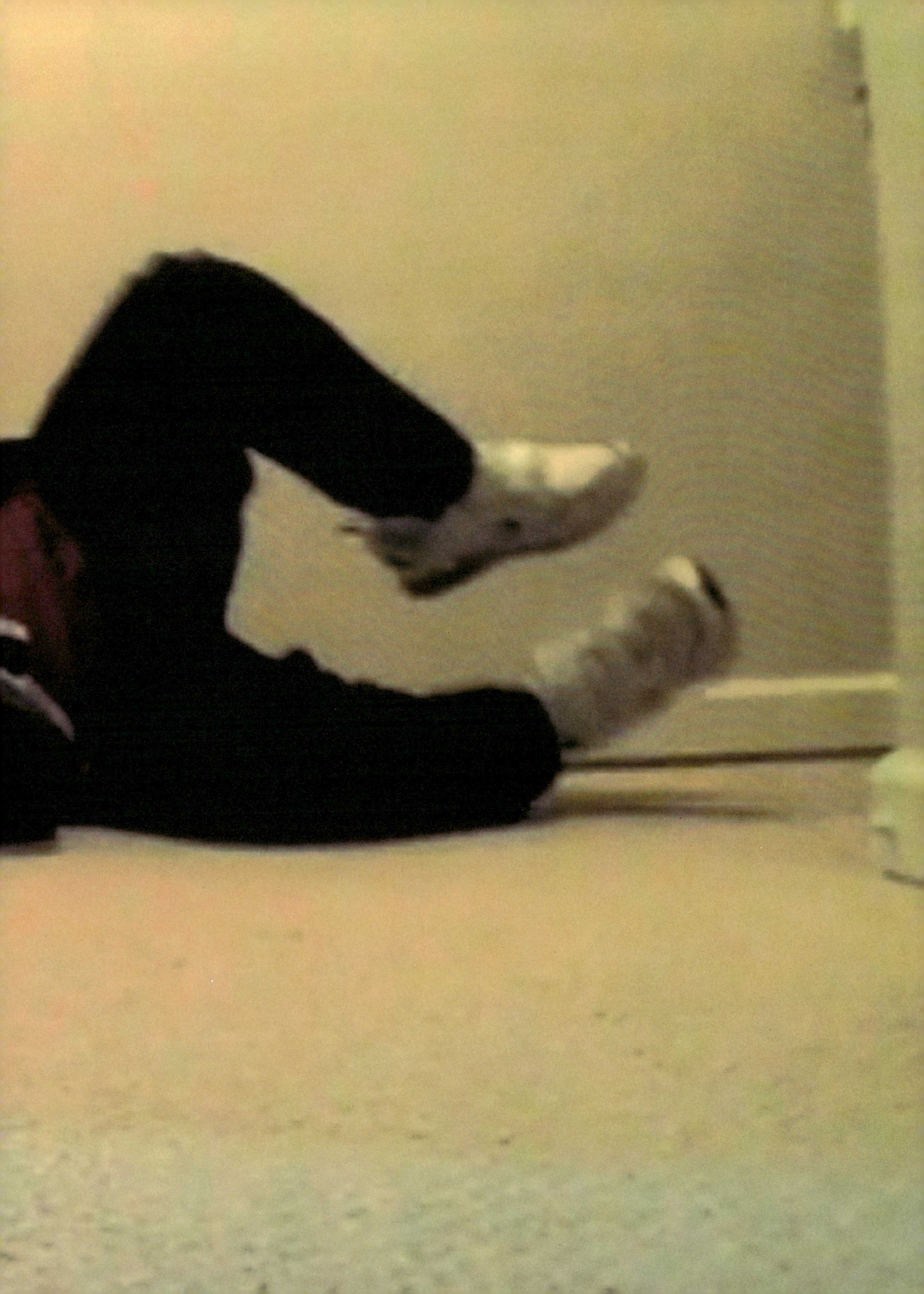

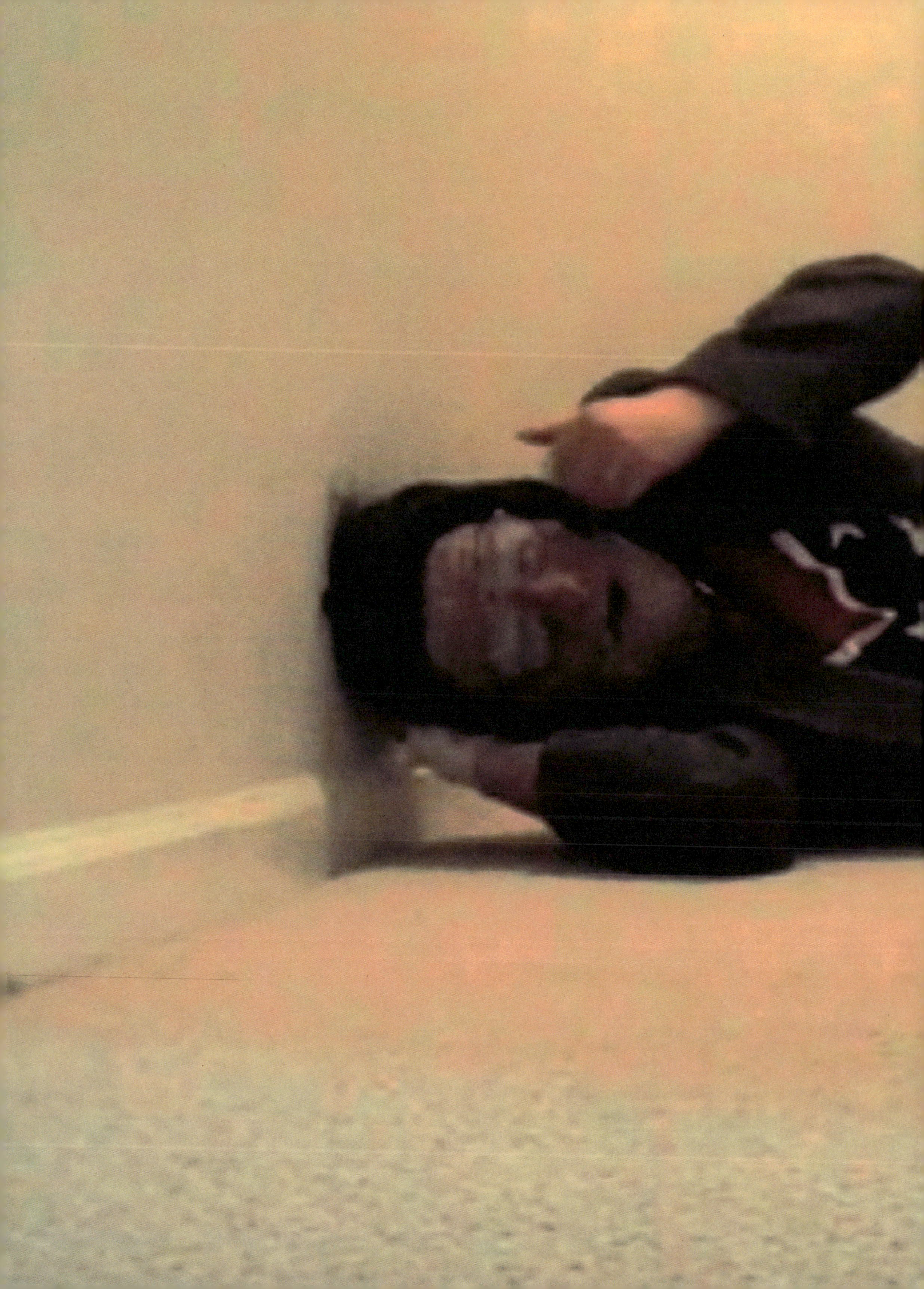

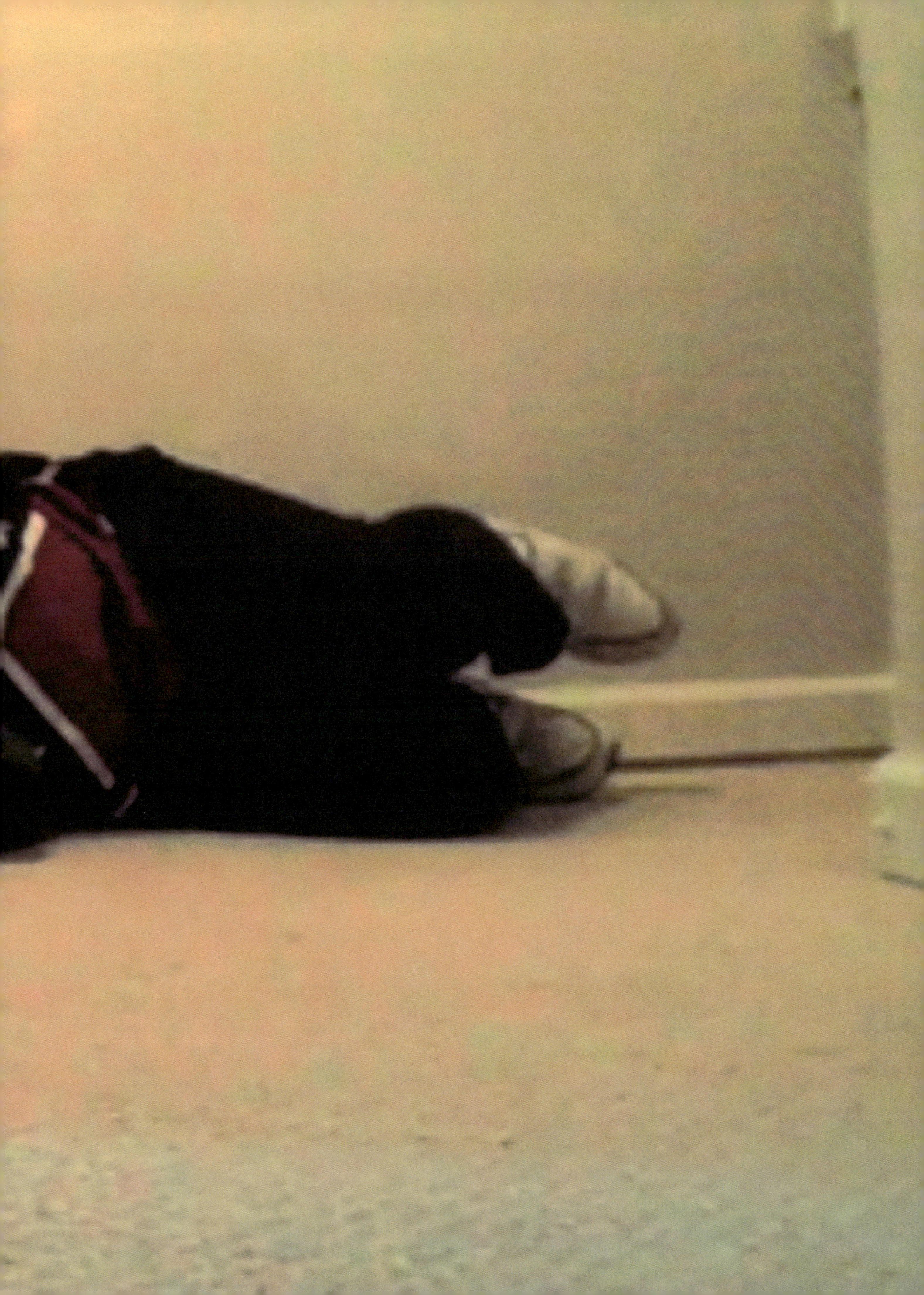

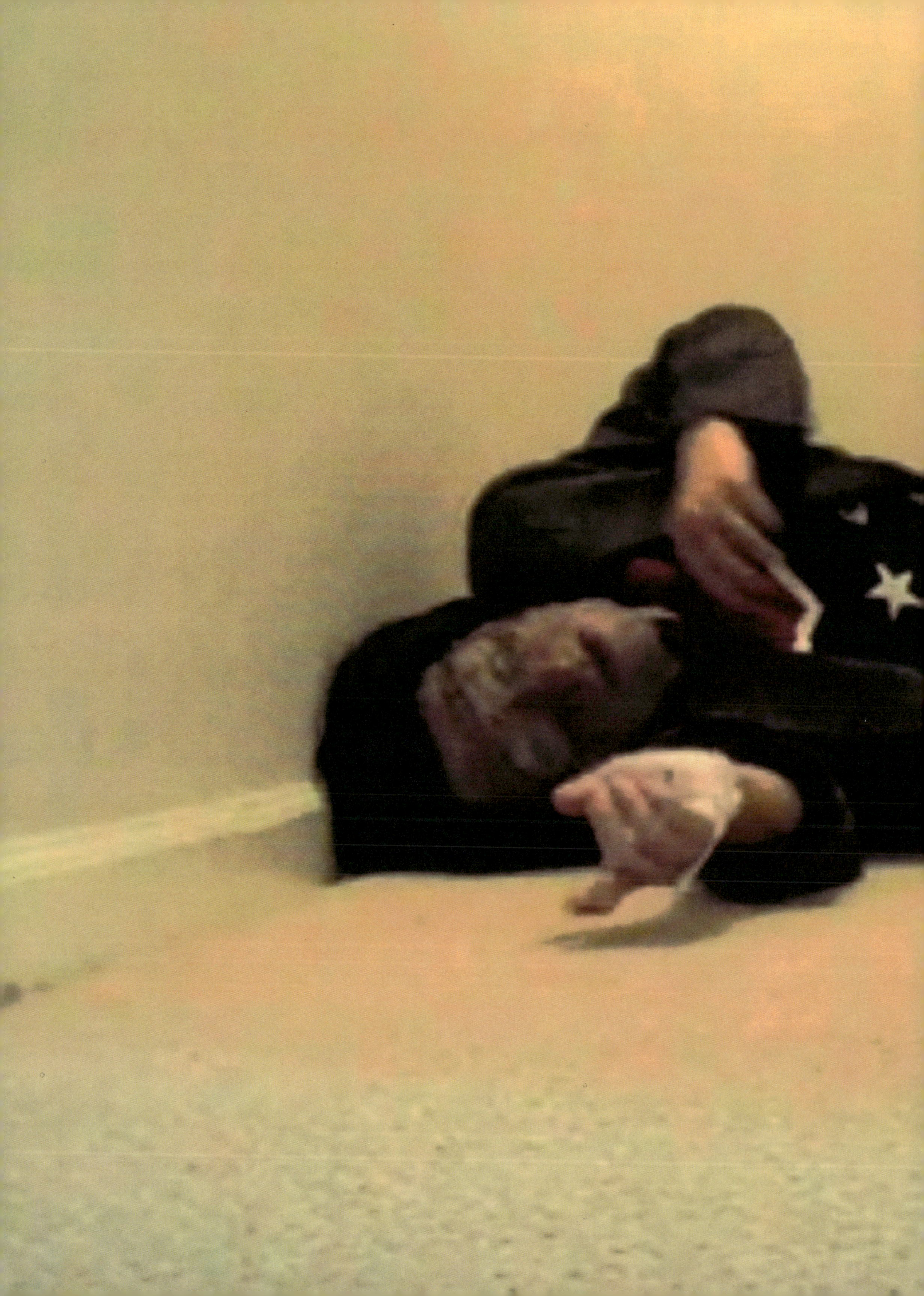

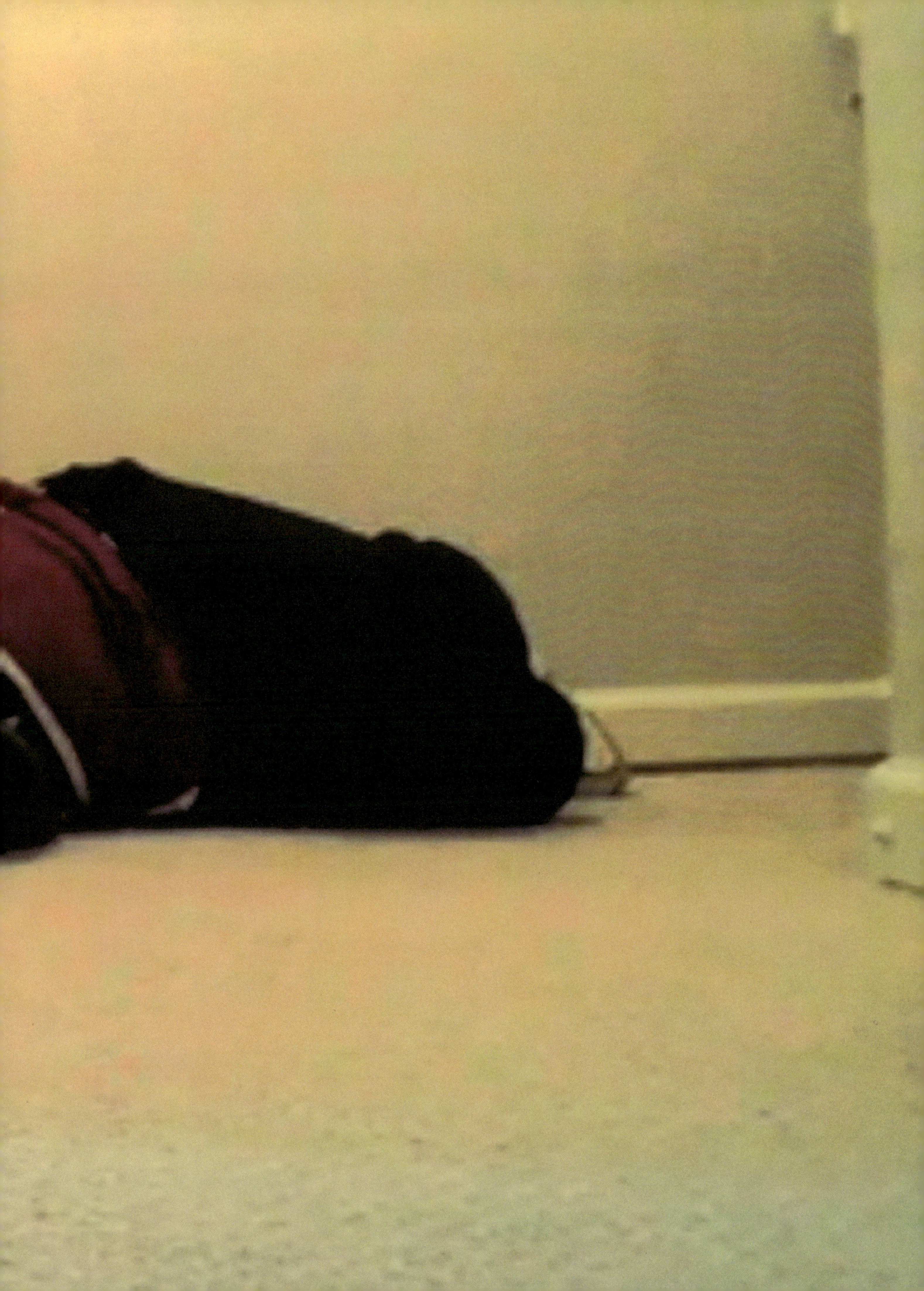

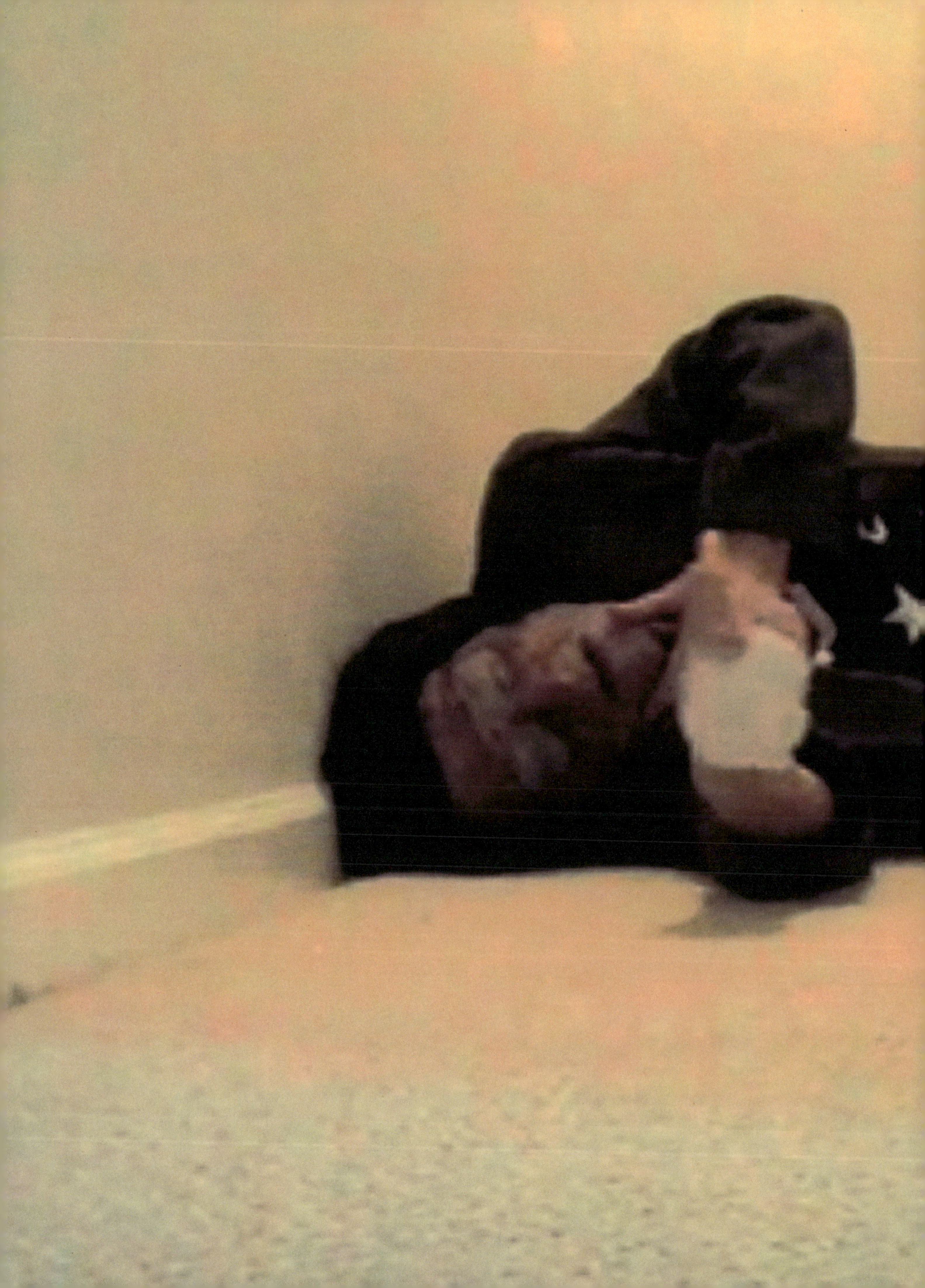

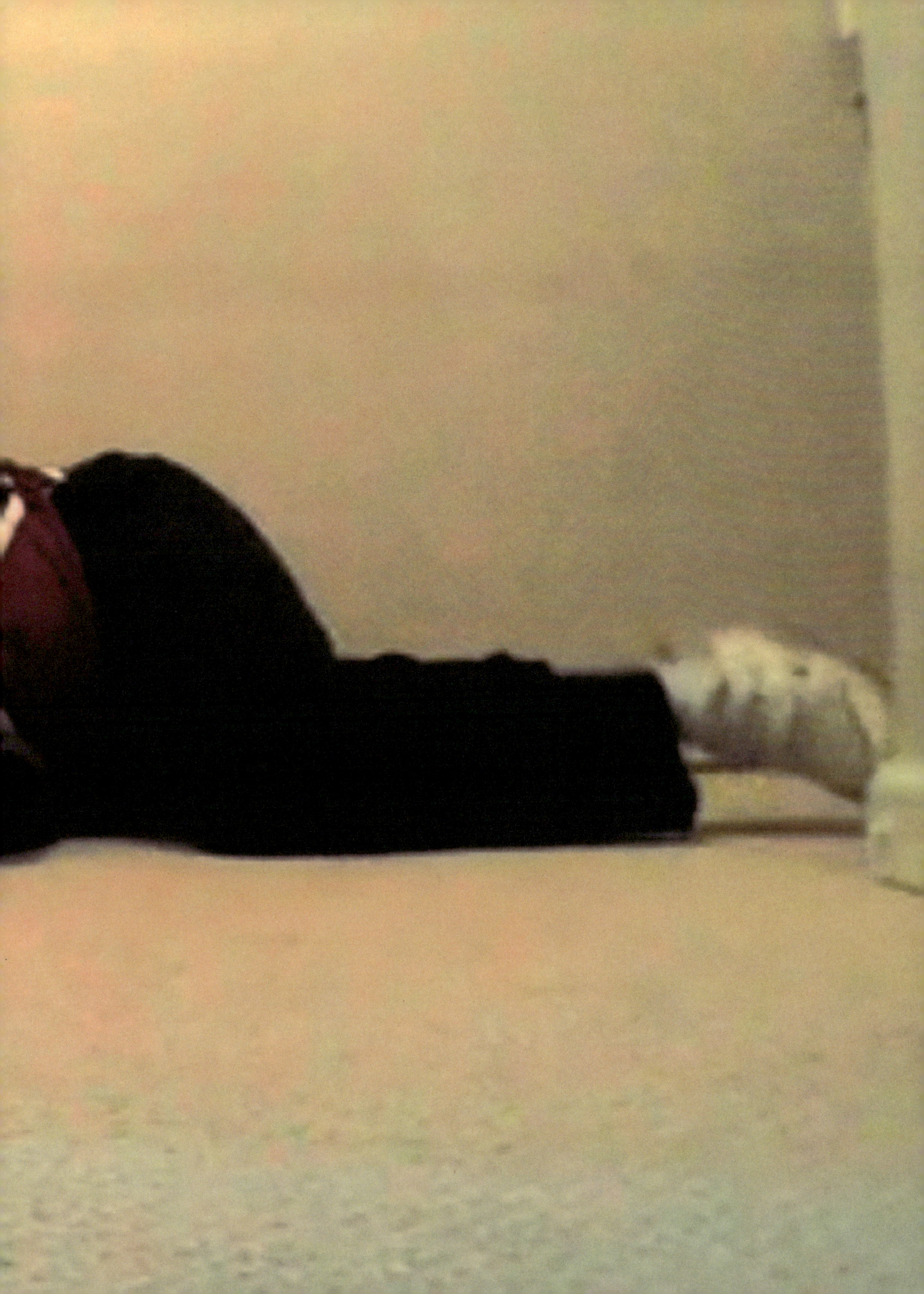

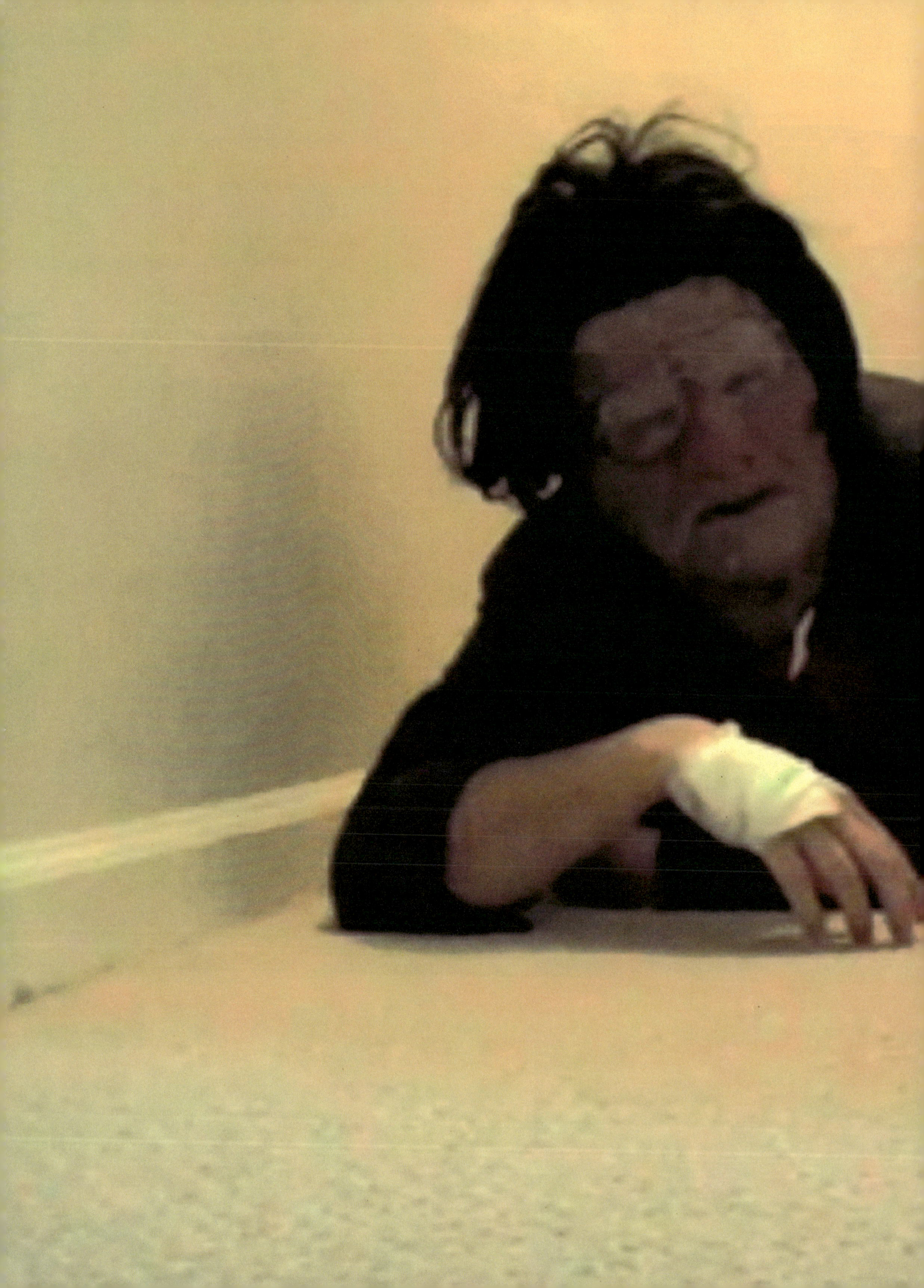

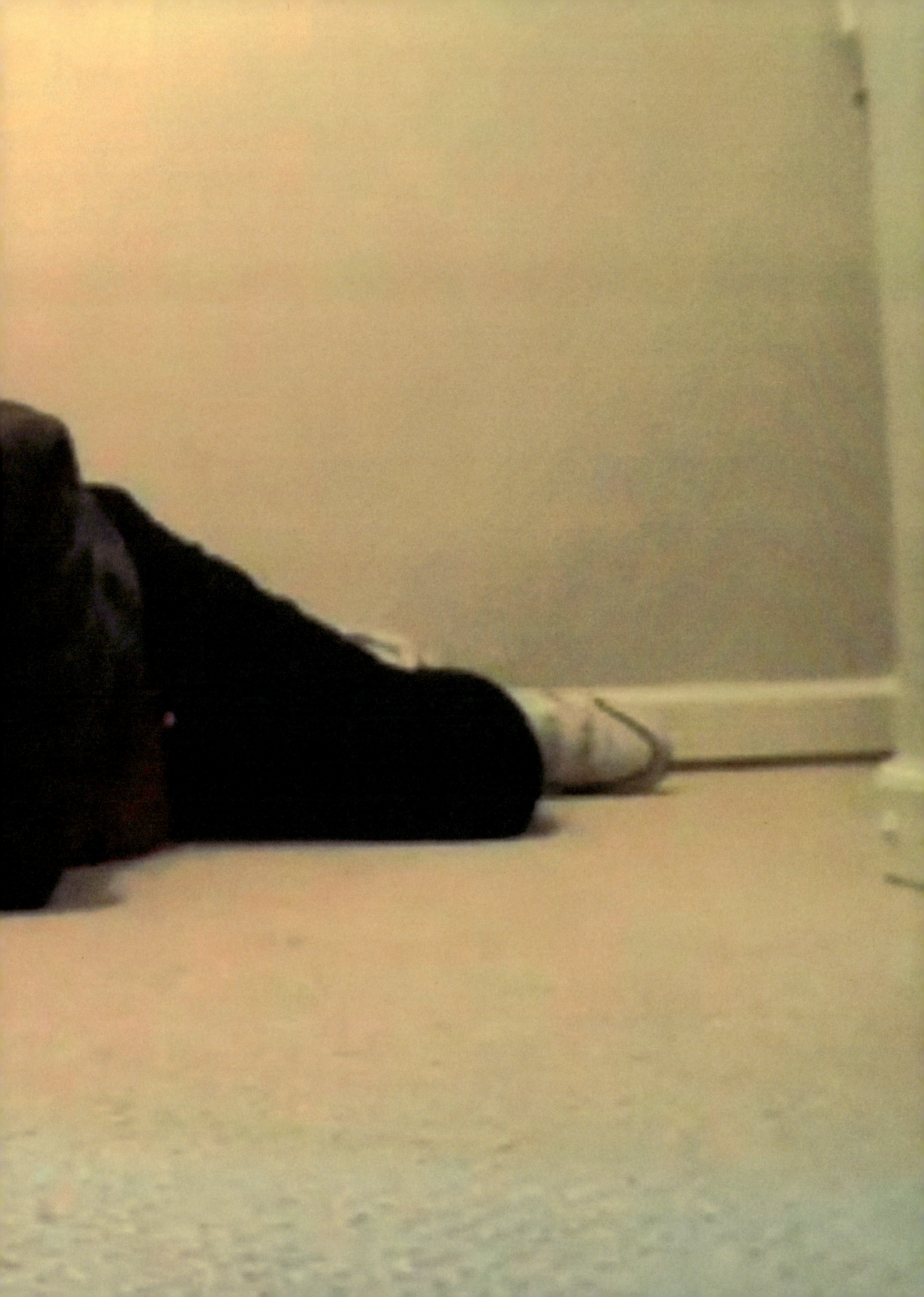

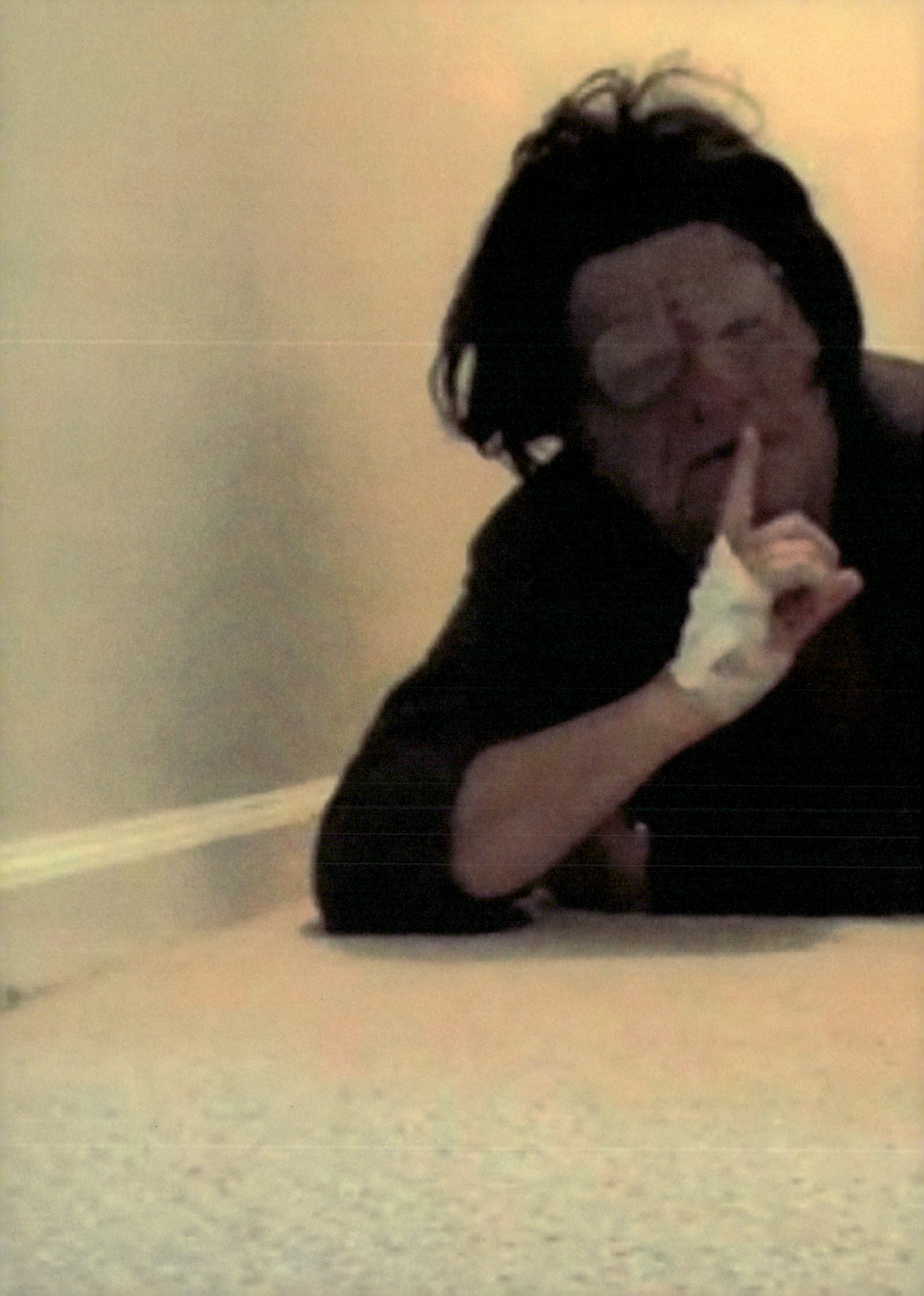

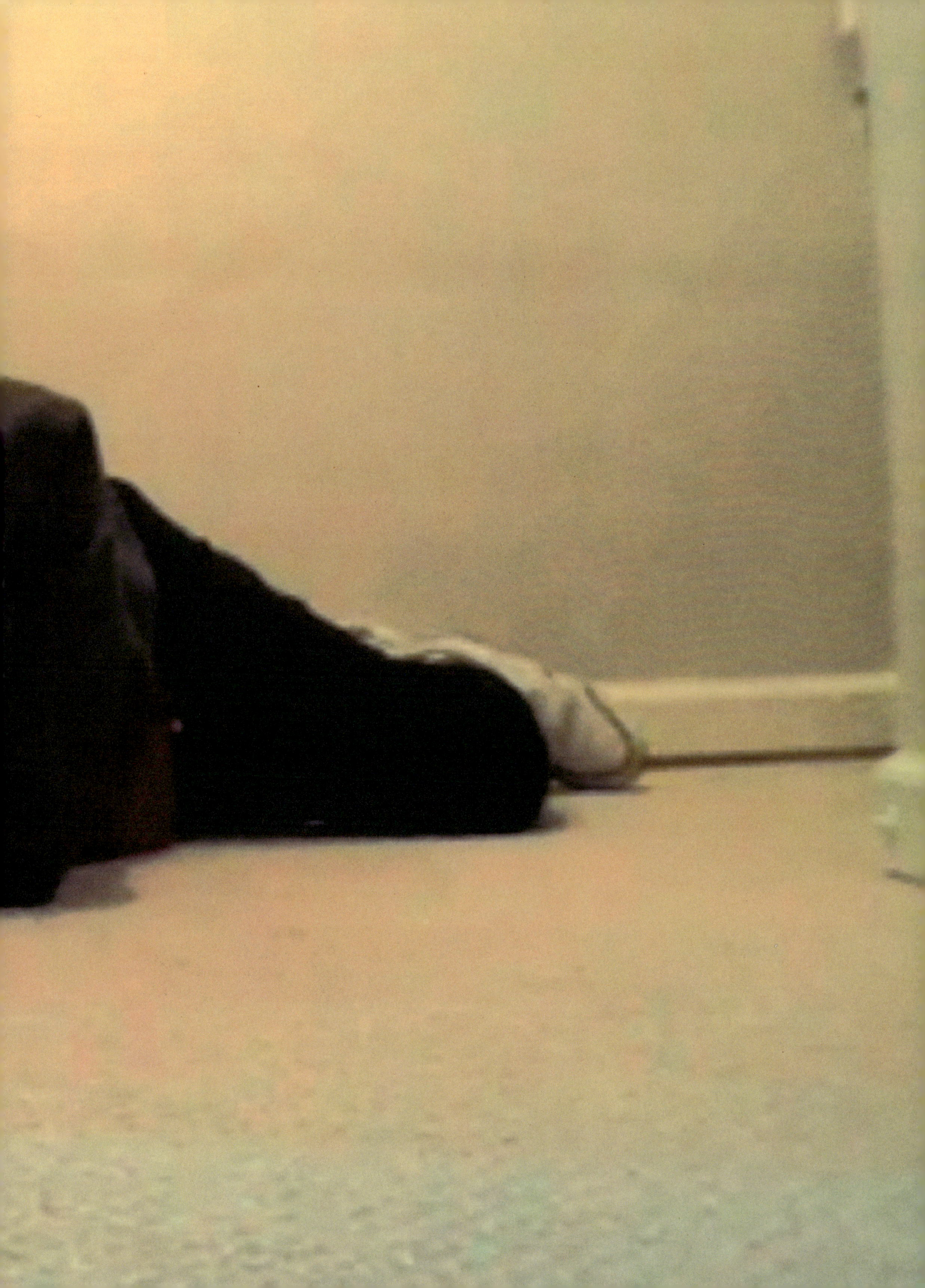

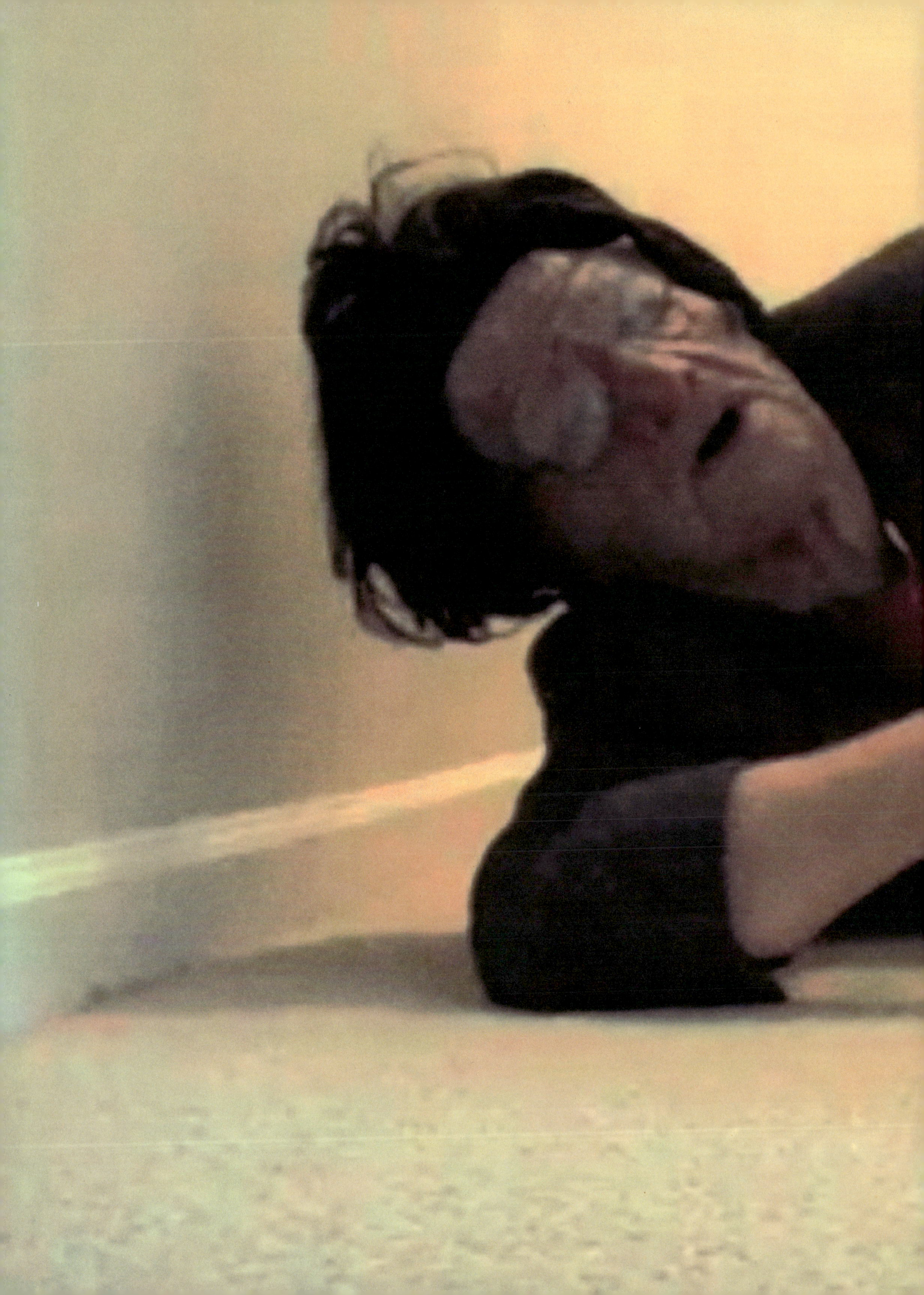

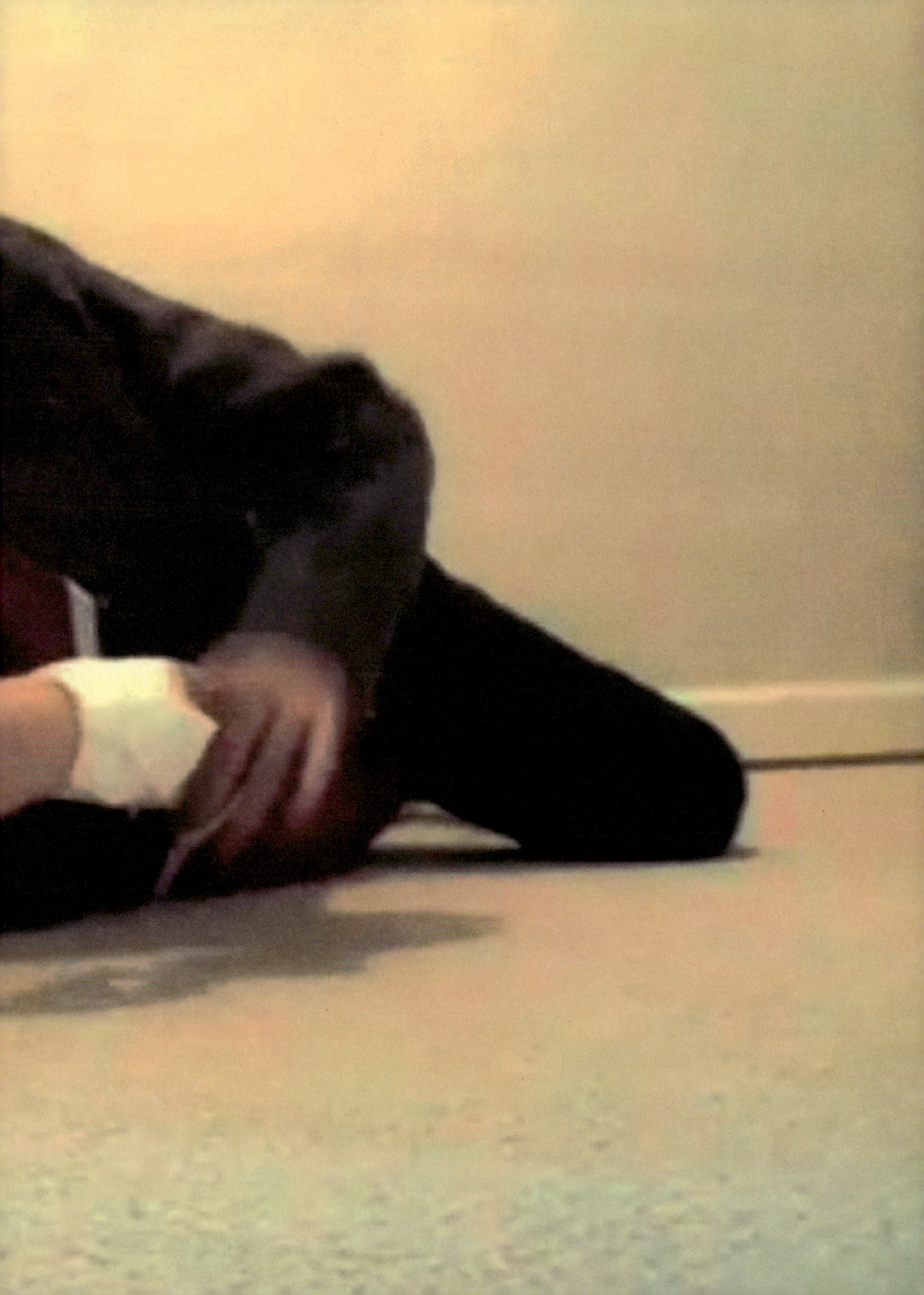

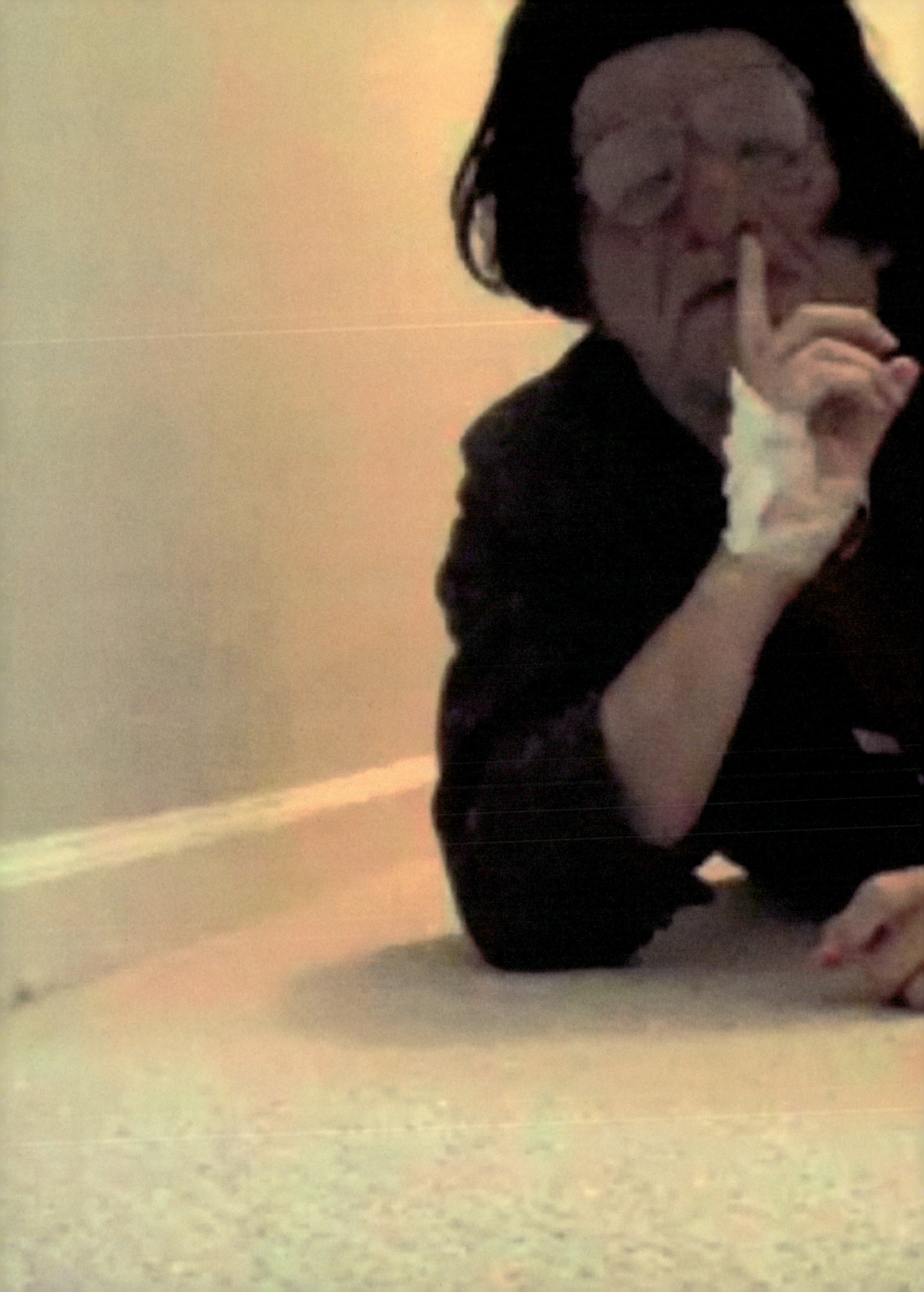

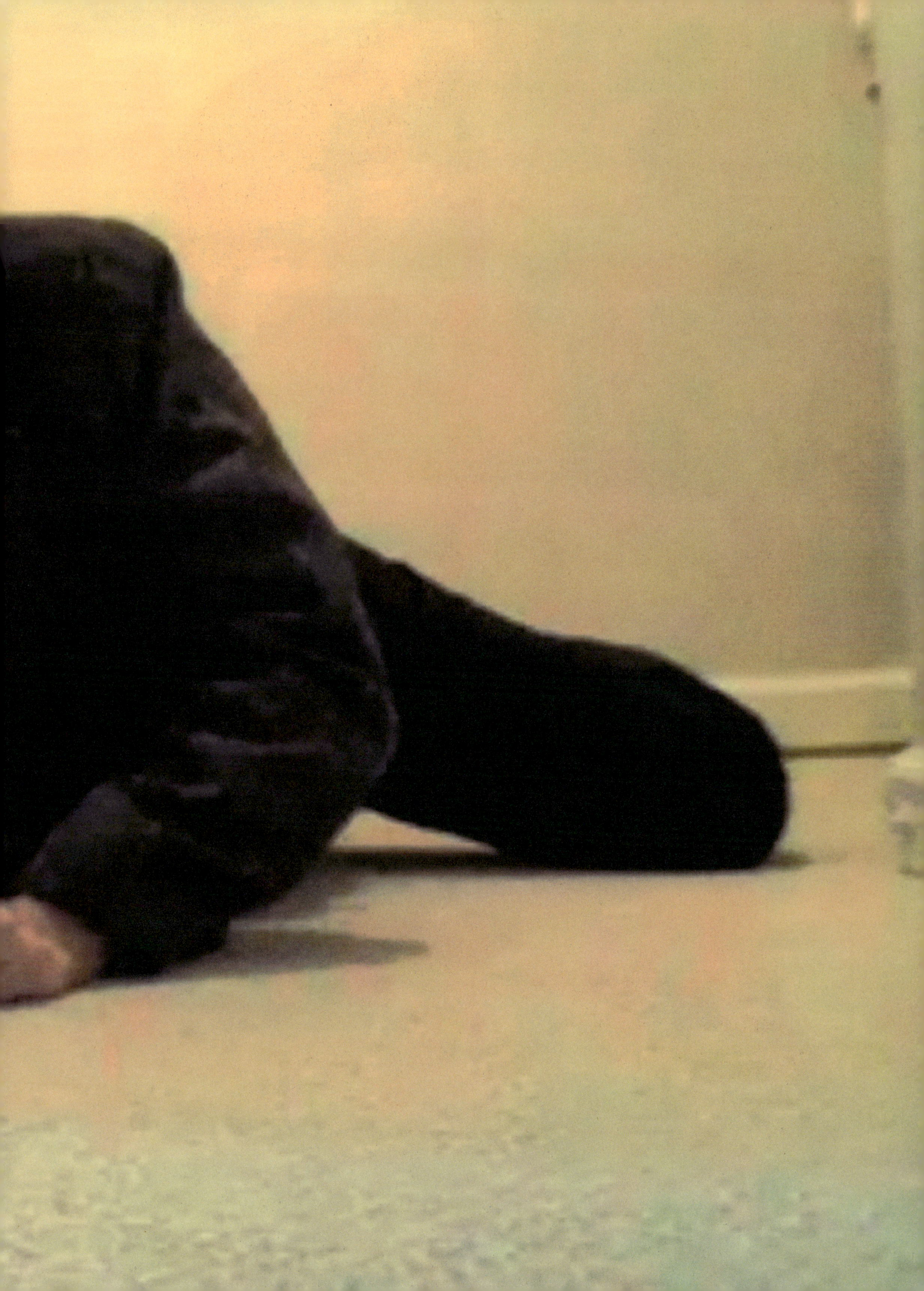

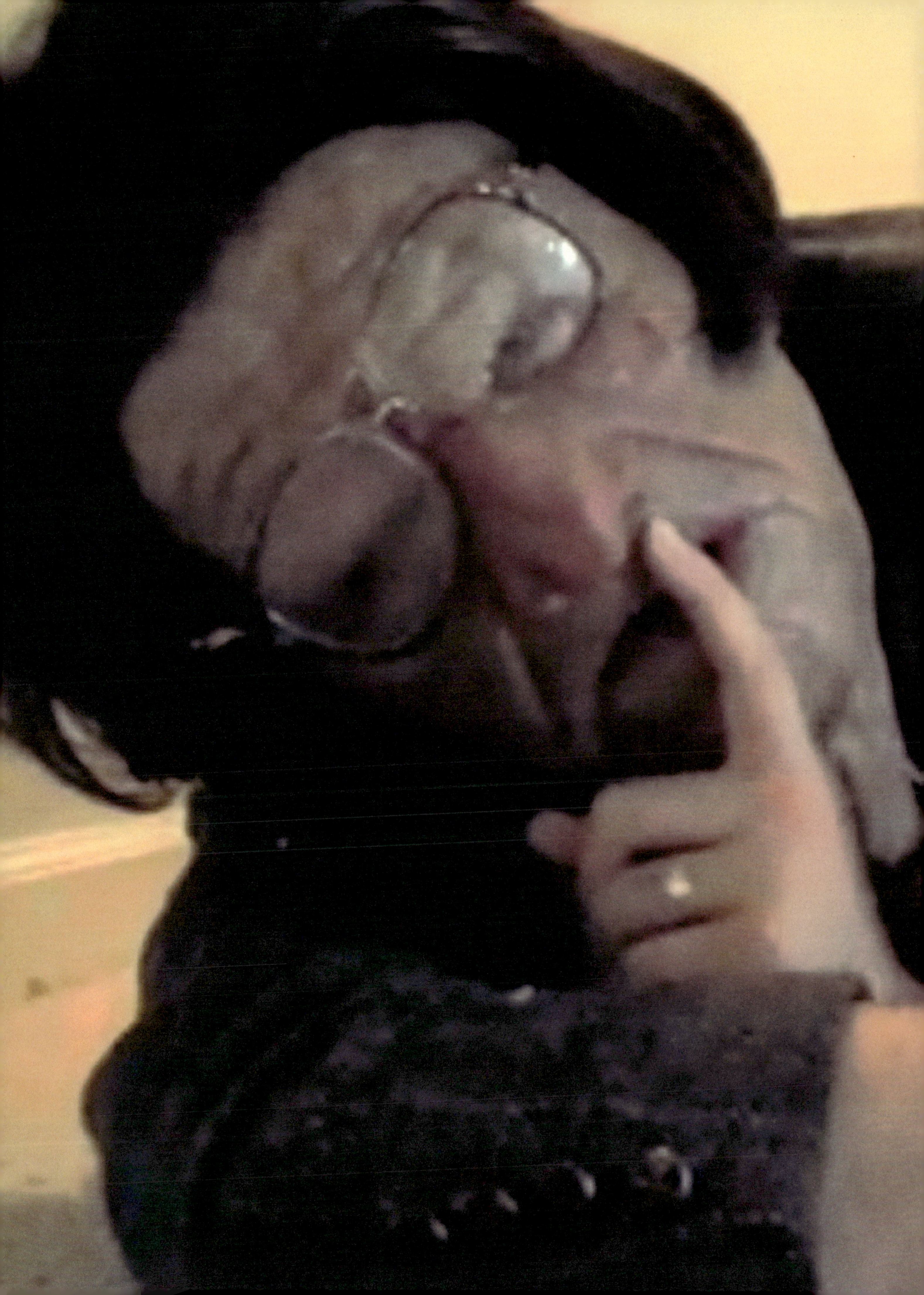

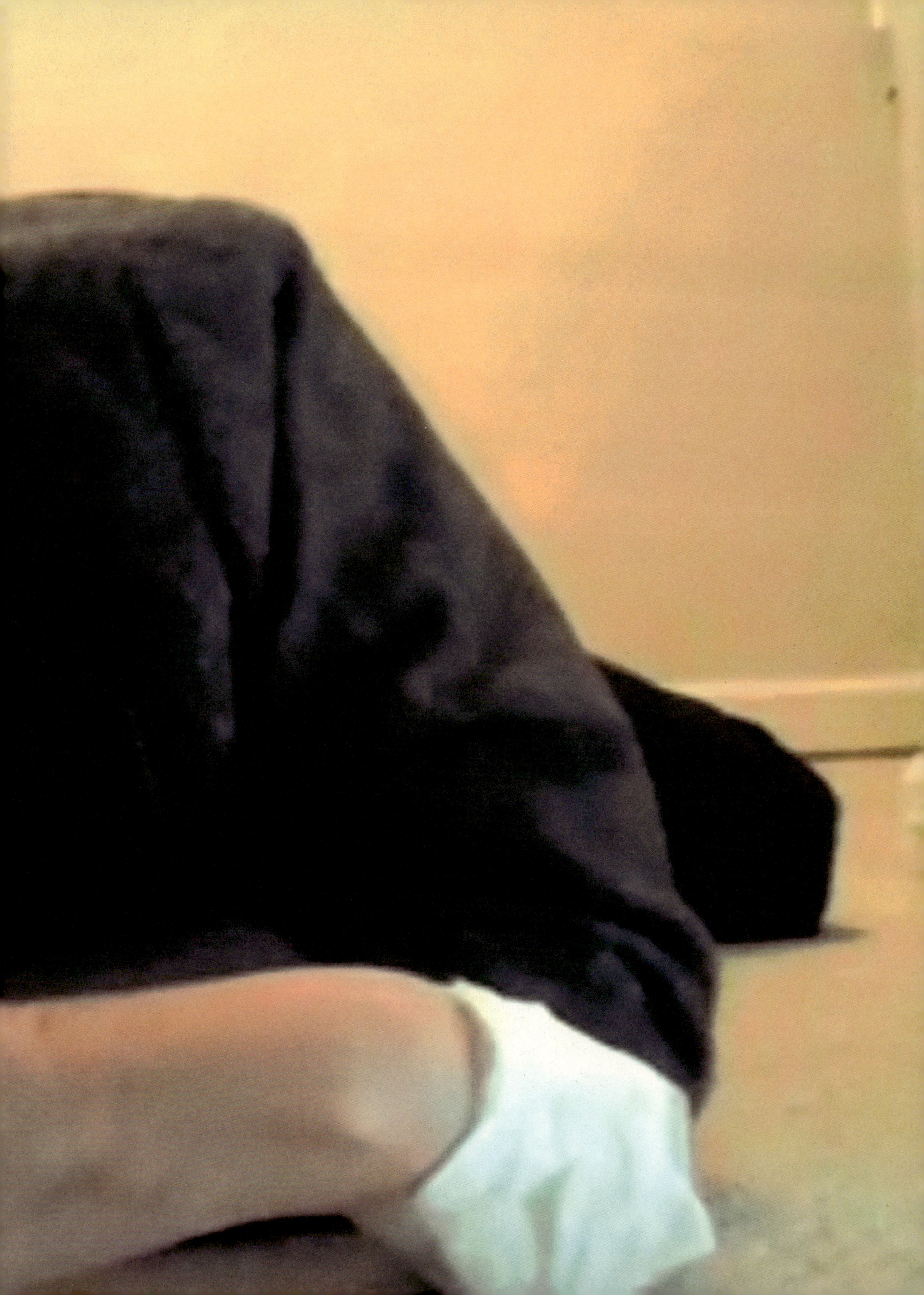

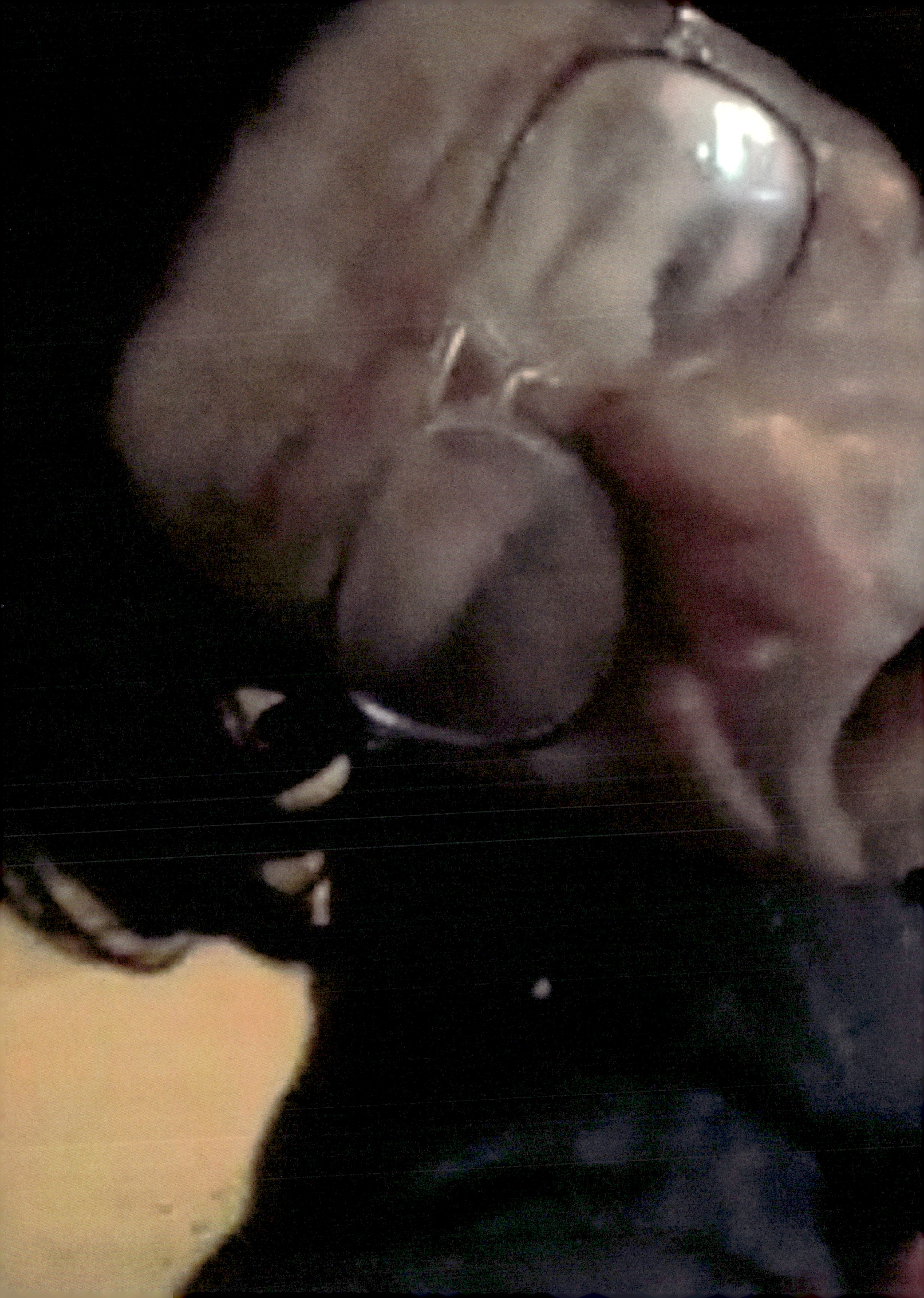

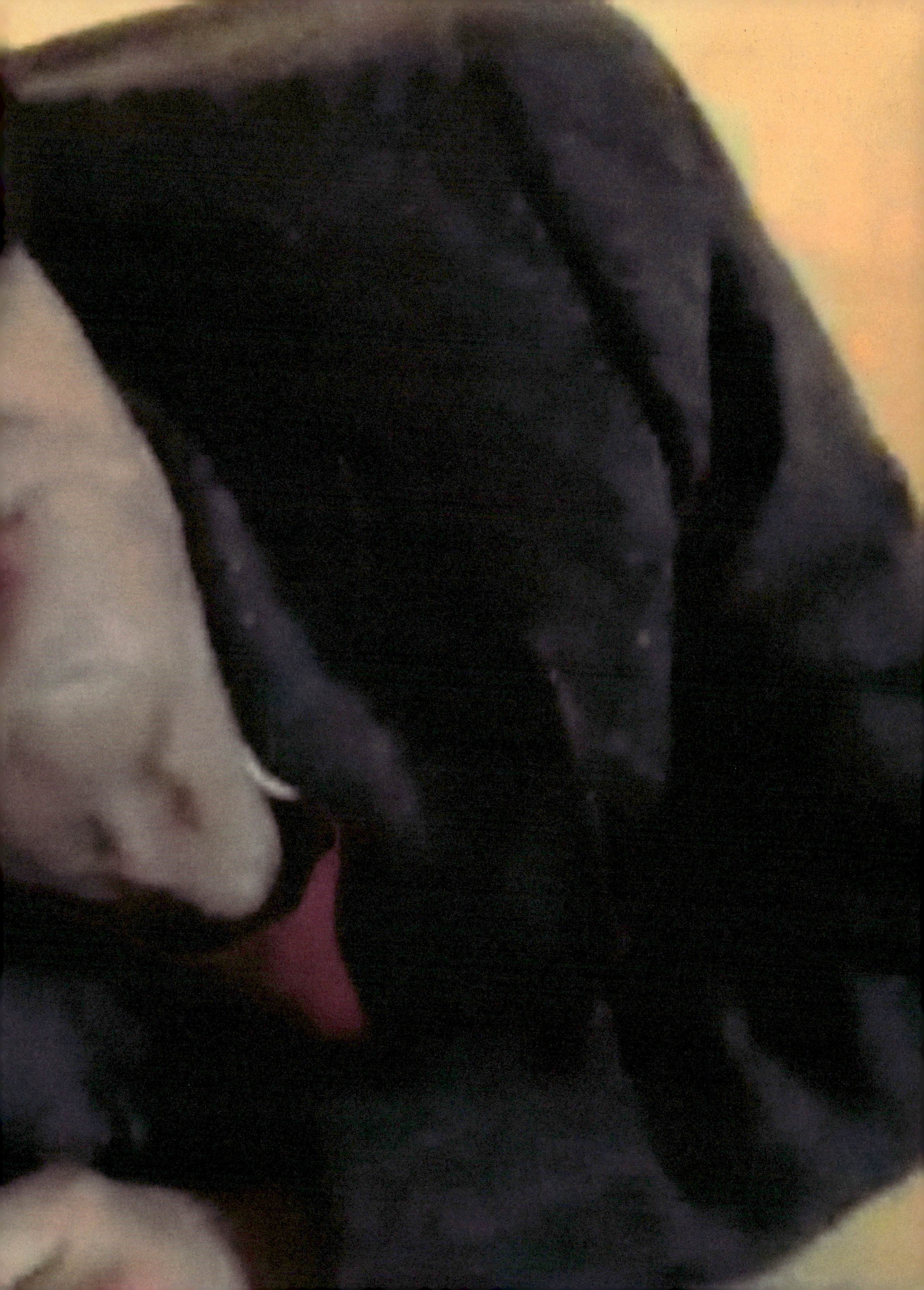

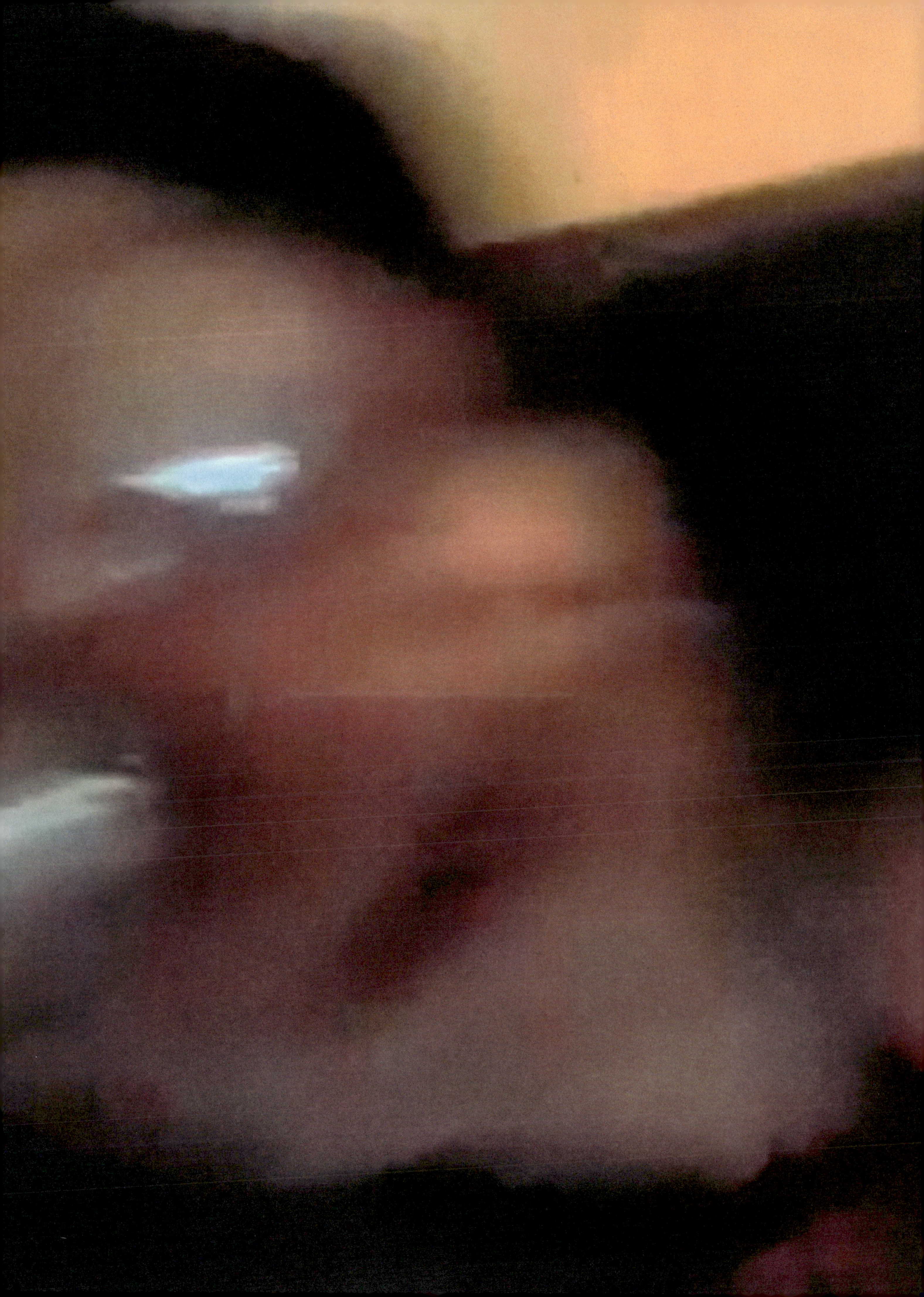

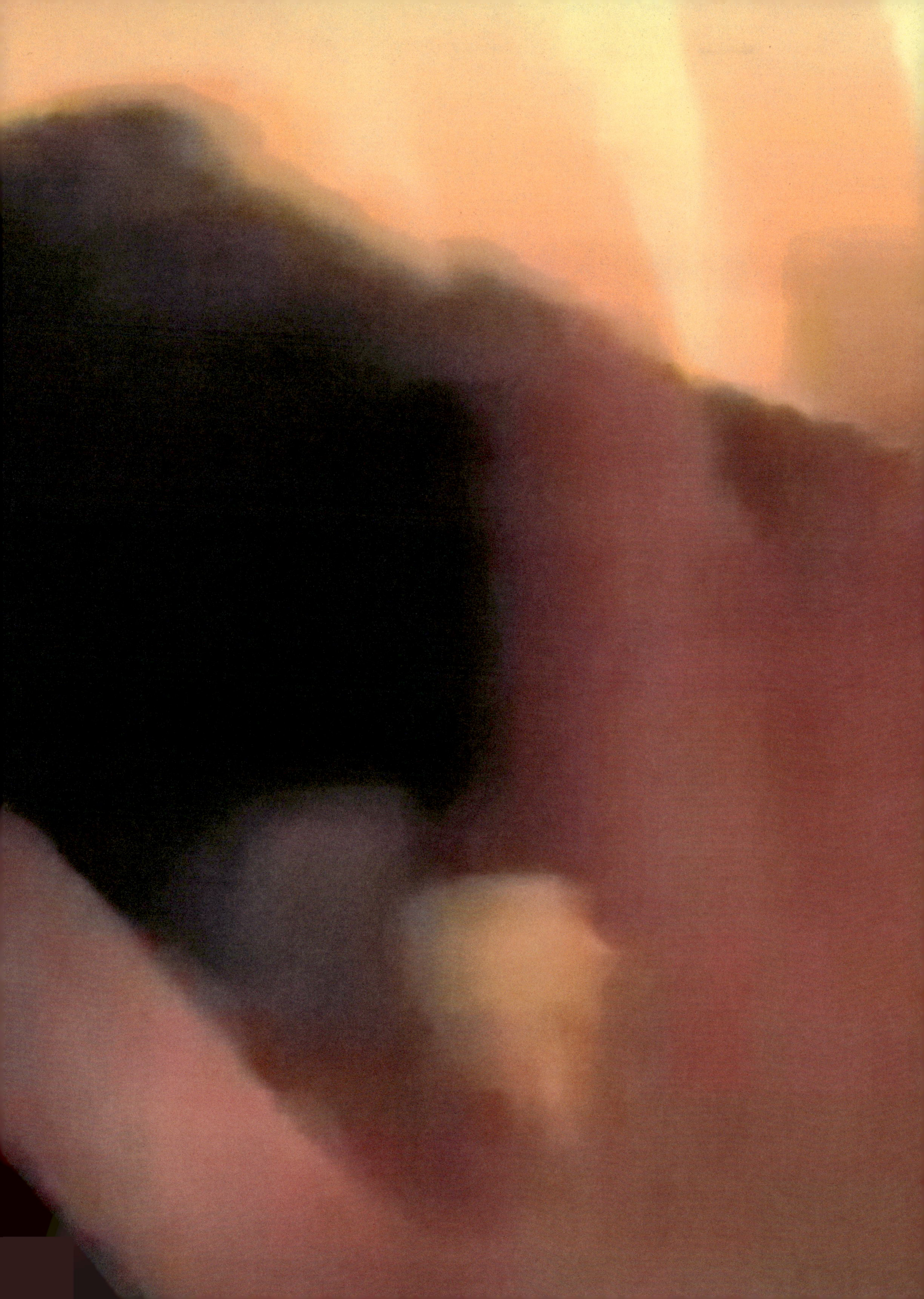

PRECEDING:

Deleted scenes from the film
Trash Humpers (2009)
Still sequence from 14:43–16:44.
Director, writer Harmony Korine;
Editing Leo Scott; Starring Paul
Booker, Dave Cloud, and Chris
Crofton, et al; Produced by
Alcove Entertainment, agnès b.

Trouble is Comin, 2010
Acrylic medium on vinyl, enamel
spray paint and ink on canvas
117 x 60 inches
Courtesy of the Artists and
Andrea Rosen Gallery, New York

STAPLED INSERT:

Untitled, 2009
Three typewritten pages by
Harmony Korine
8½ x 11 inches
Courtesy of the Artist

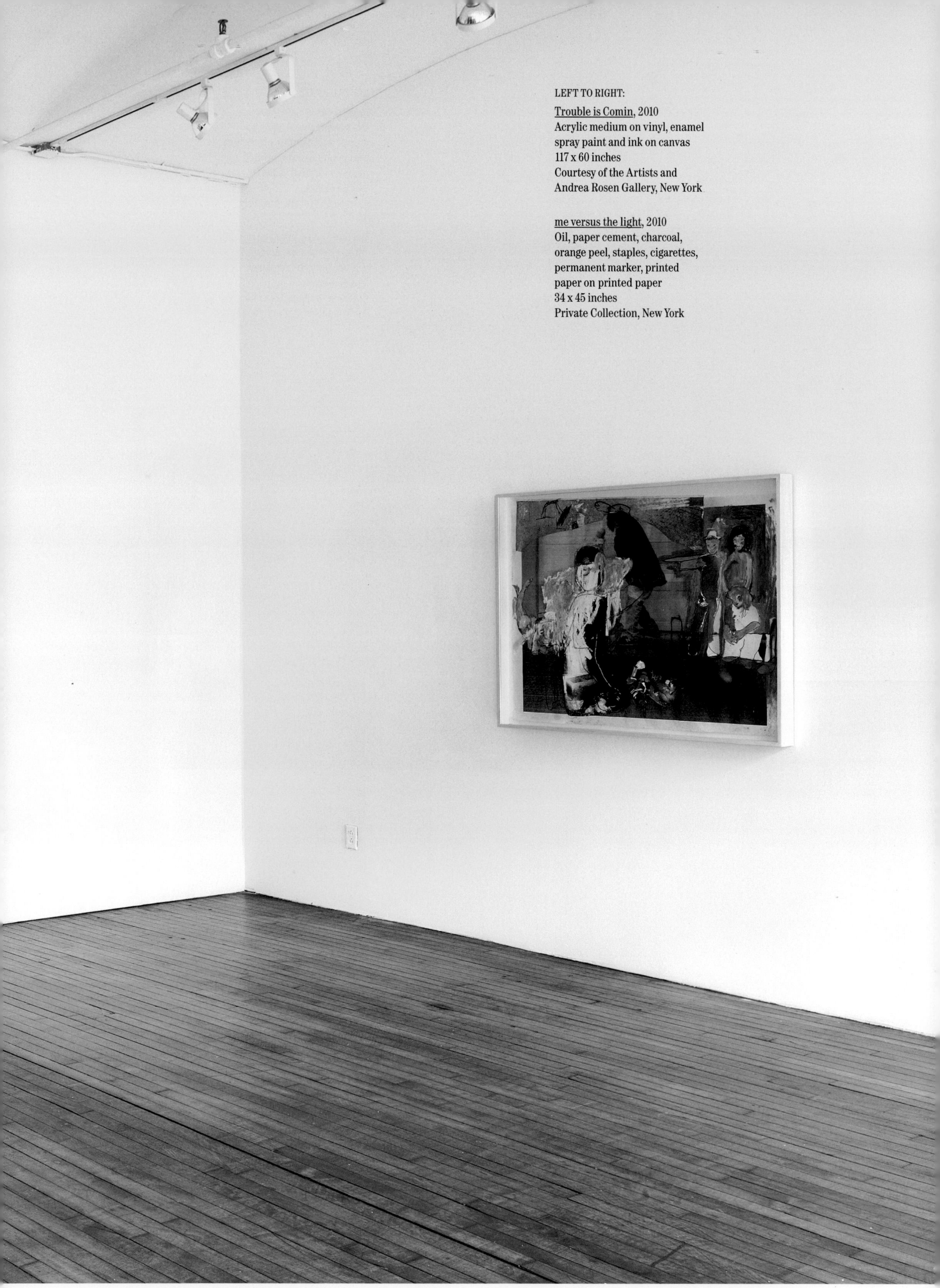

LEFT TO RIGHT:

Trouble is Comin, 2010
Acrylic medium on vinyl, enamel spray paint and ink on canvas
117 x 60 inches
Courtesy of the Artists and Andrea Rosen Gallery, New York

me versus the light, 2010
Oil, paper cement, charcoal, orange peel, staples, cigarettes, permanent marker, printed paper on printed paper
34 x 45 inches
Private Collection, New York

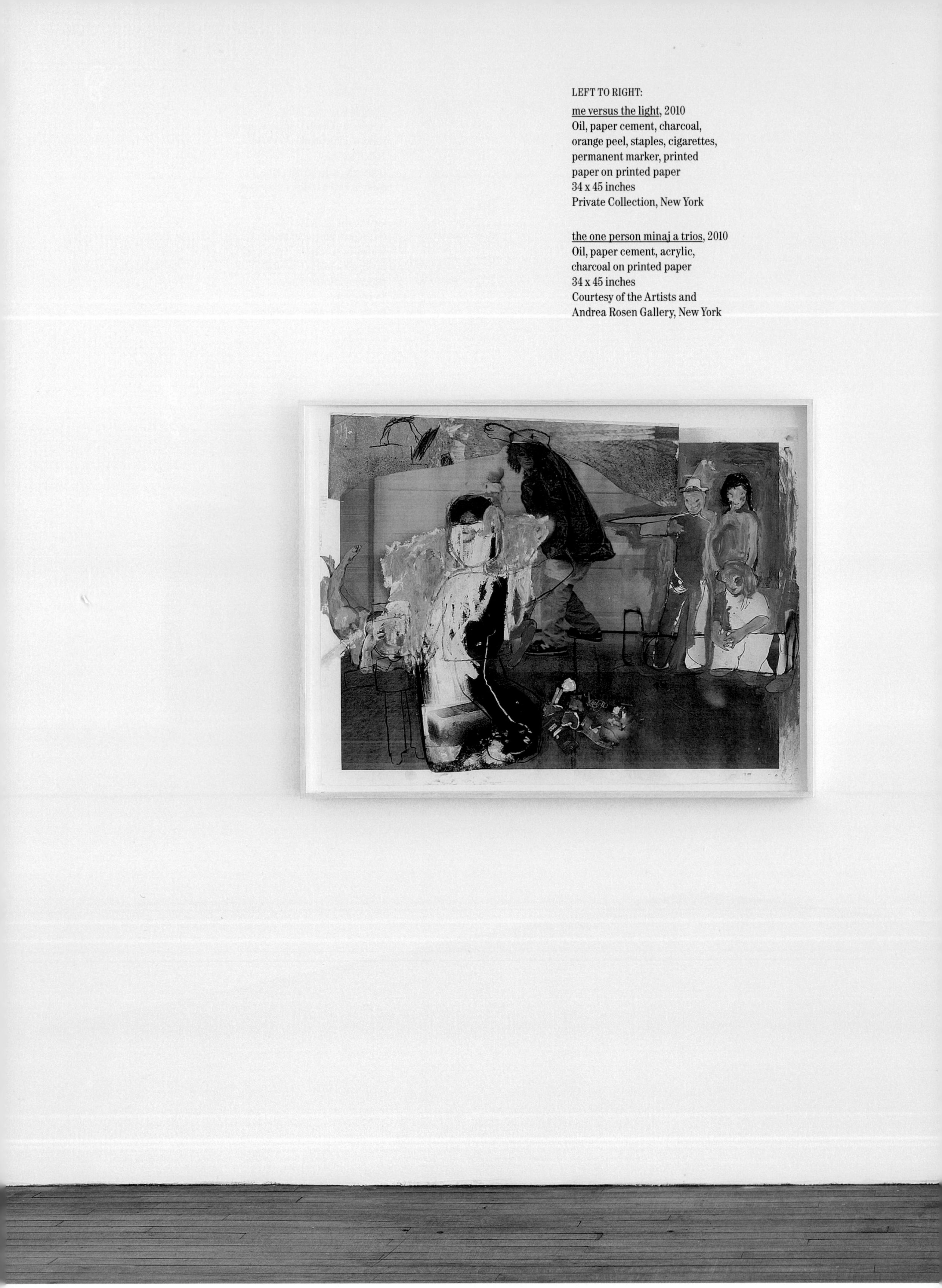

LEFT TO RIGHT:

me versus the light, 2010
Oil, paper cement, charcoal, orange peel, staples, cigarettes, permanent marker, printed paper on printed paper
34 x 45 inches
Private Collection, New York

the one person minaj a trios, 2010
Oil, paper cement, acrylic, charcoal on printed paper
34 x 45 inches
Courtesy of the Artists and Andrea Rosen Gallery, New York

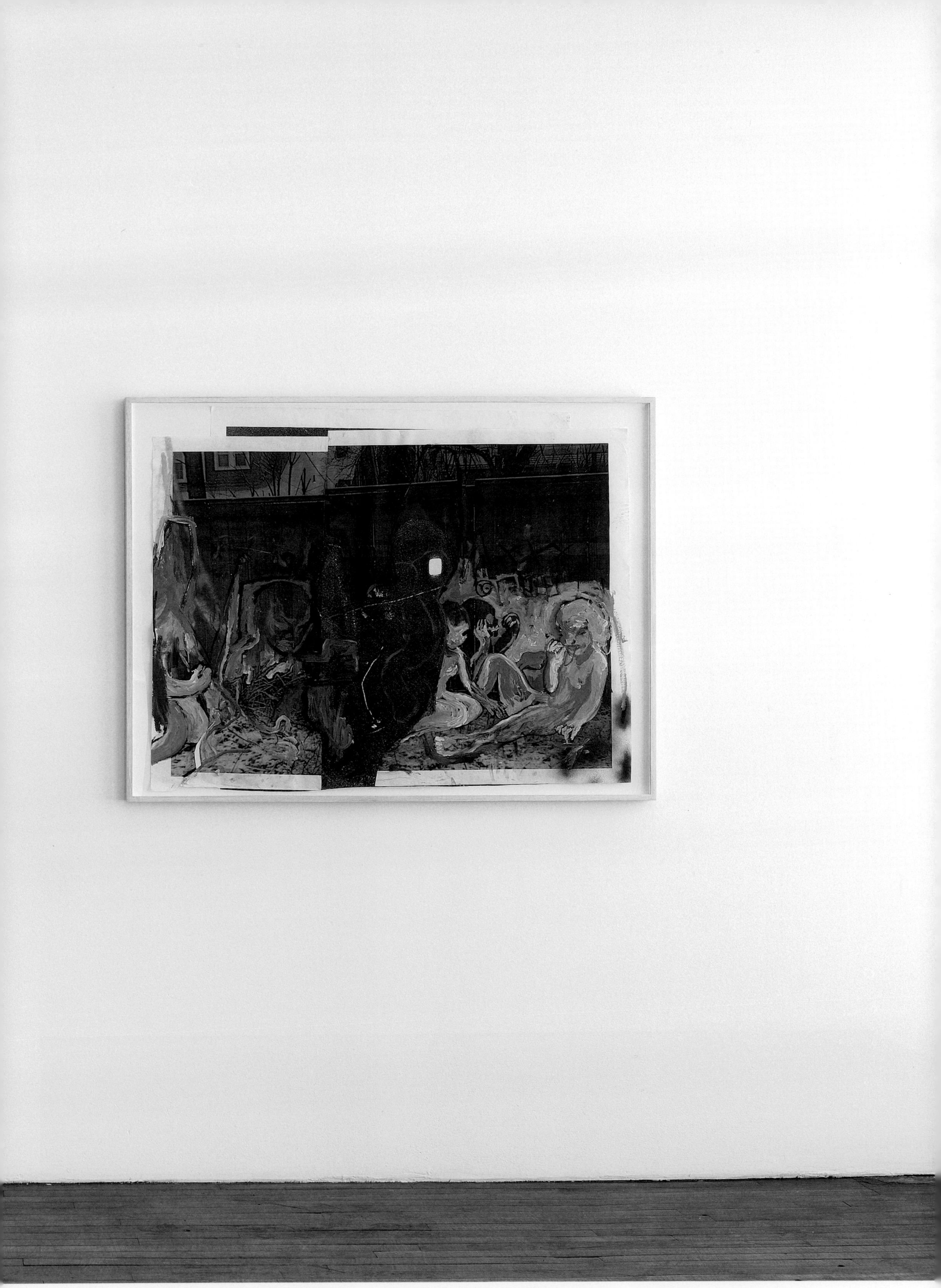

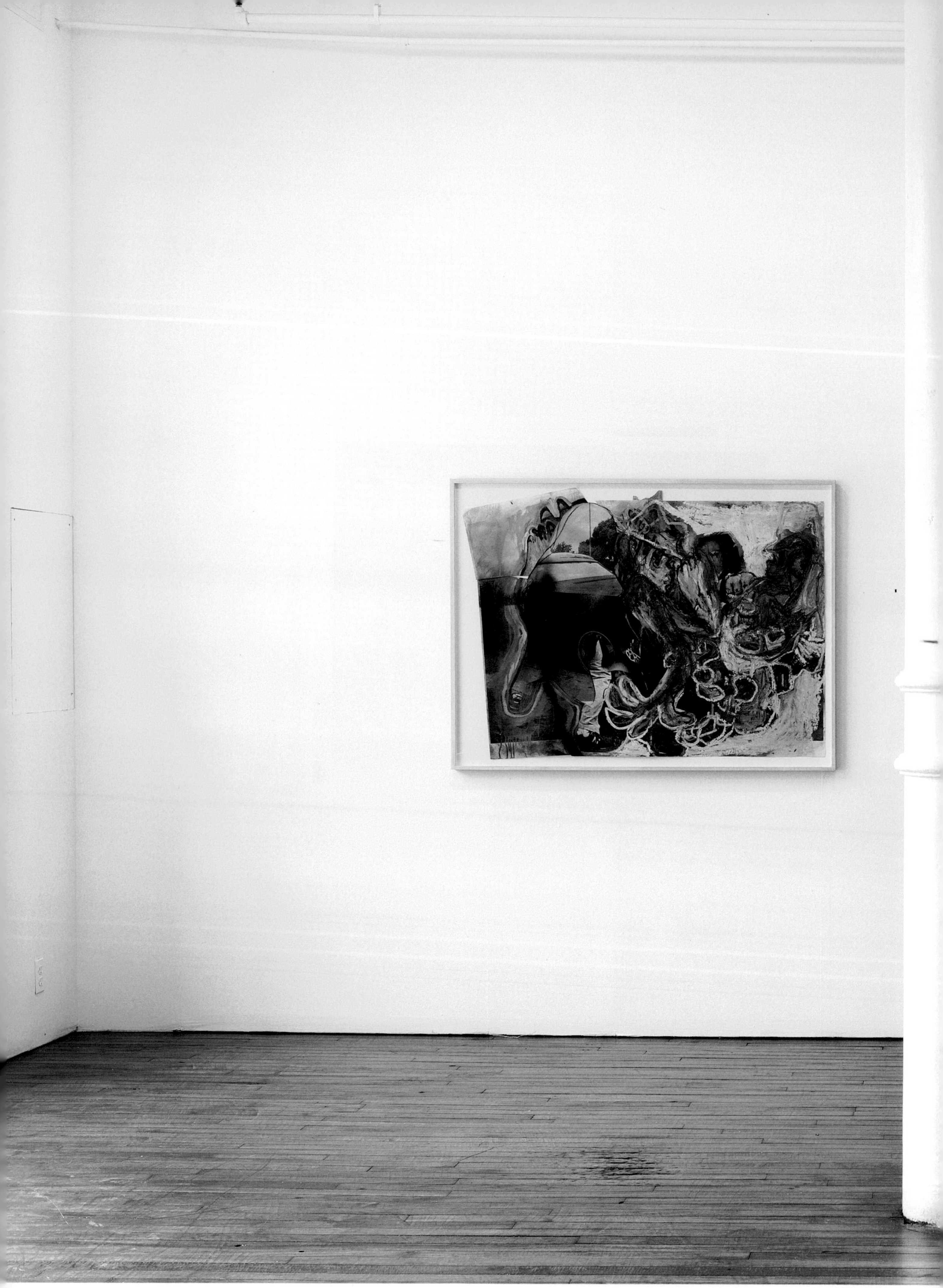

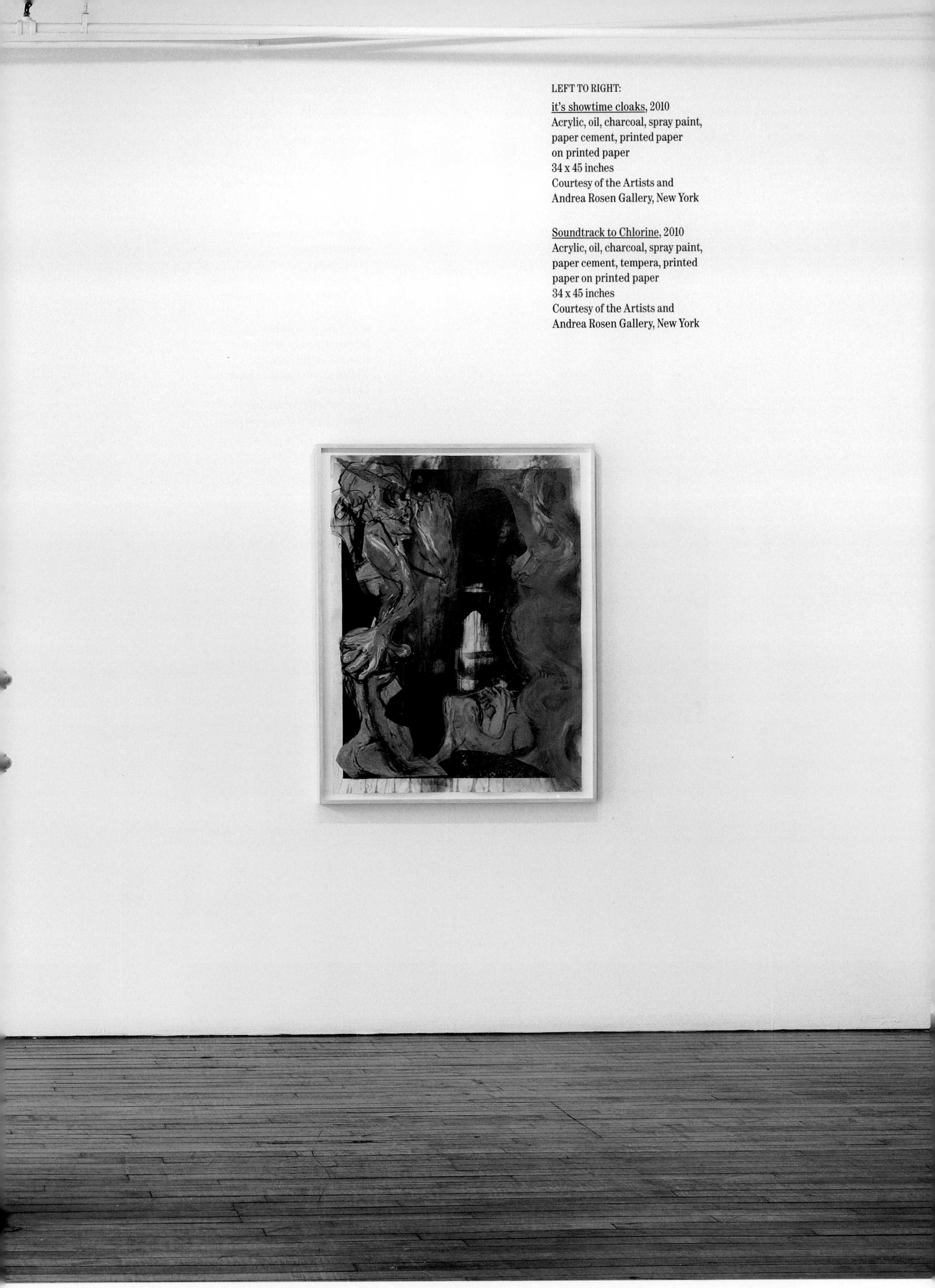

LEFT TO RIGHT:

it's showtime cloaks, 2010
Acrylic, oil, charcoal, spray paint, paper cement, printed paper on printed paper
34 x 45 inches
Courtesy of the Artists and Andrea Rosen Gallery, New York

Soundtrack to Chlorine, 2010
Acrylic, oil, charcoal, spray paint, paper cement, tempera, printed paper on printed paper
34 x 45 inches
Courtesy of the Artists and Andrea Rosen Gallery, New York

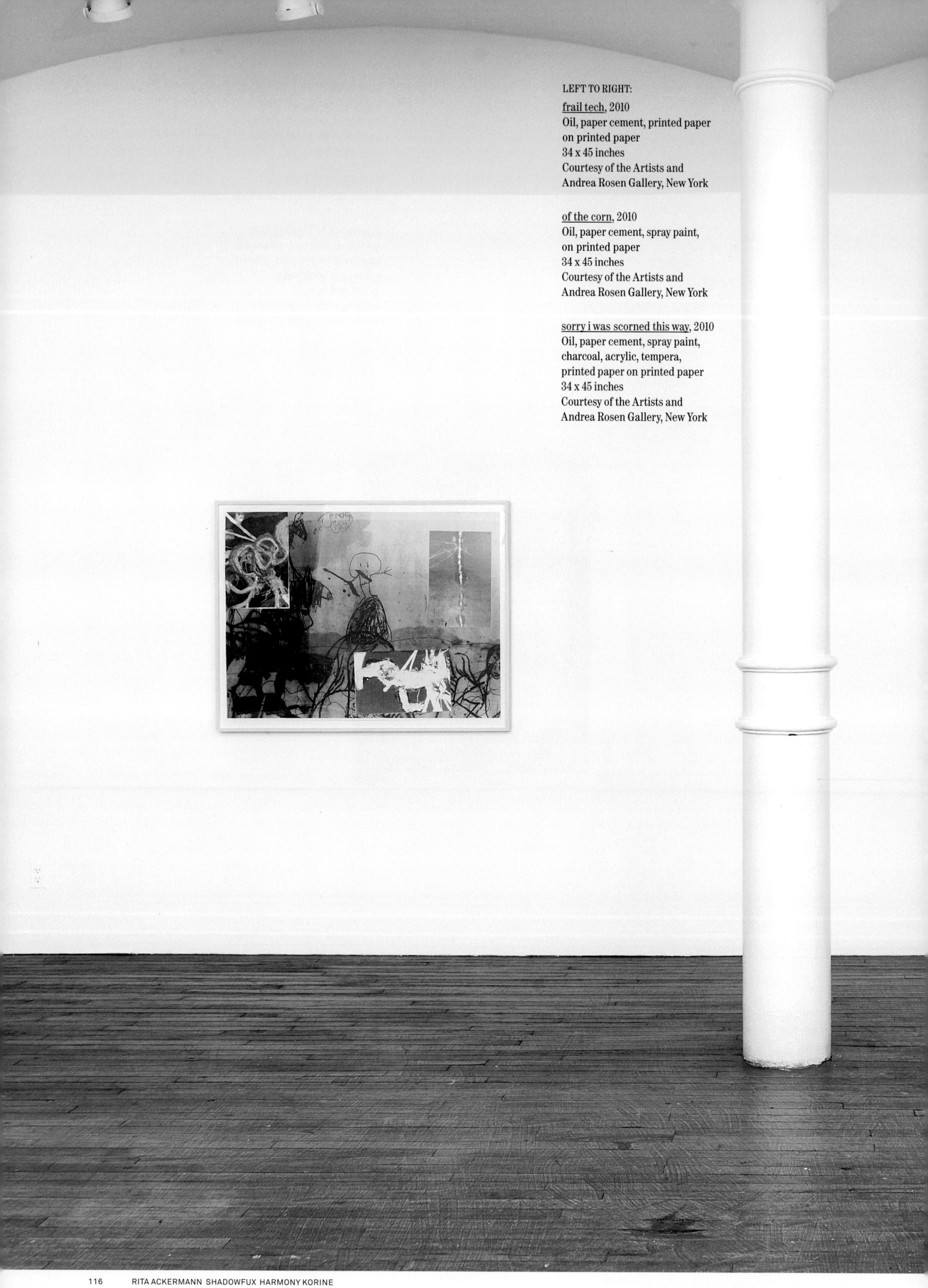

LEFT TO RIGHT:

frail tech, 2010
Oil, paper cement, printed paper
on printed paper
34 x 45 inches
Courtesy of the Artists and
Andrea Rosen Gallery, New York

of the corn, 2010
Oil, paper cement, spray paint,
on printed paper
34 x 45 inches
Courtesy of the Artists and
Andrea Rosen Gallery, New York

sorry i was scorned this way, 2010
Oil, paper cement, spray paint,
charcoal, acrylic, tempera,
printed paper on printed paper
34 x 45 inches
Courtesy of the Artists and
Andrea Rosen Gallery, New York

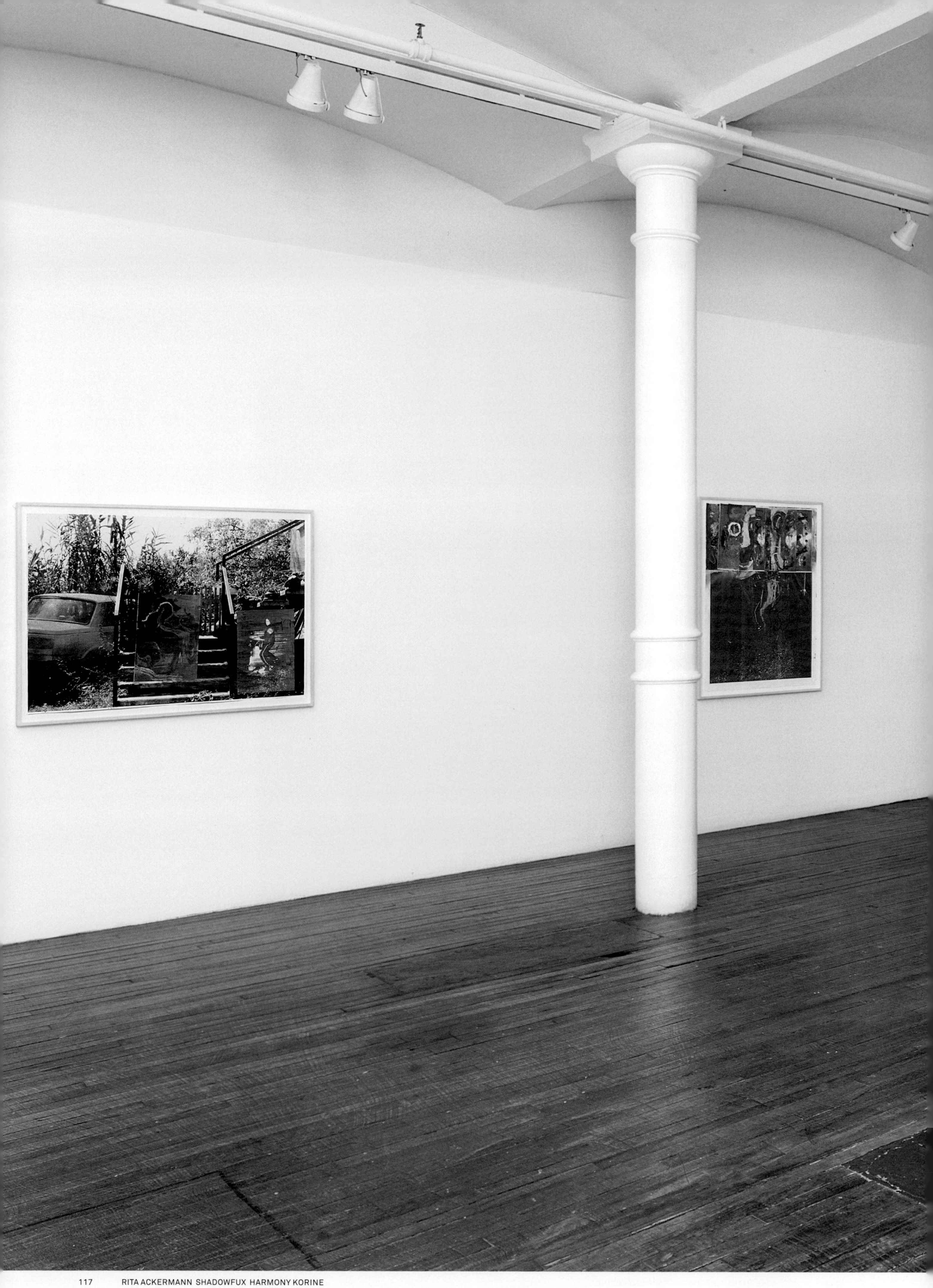

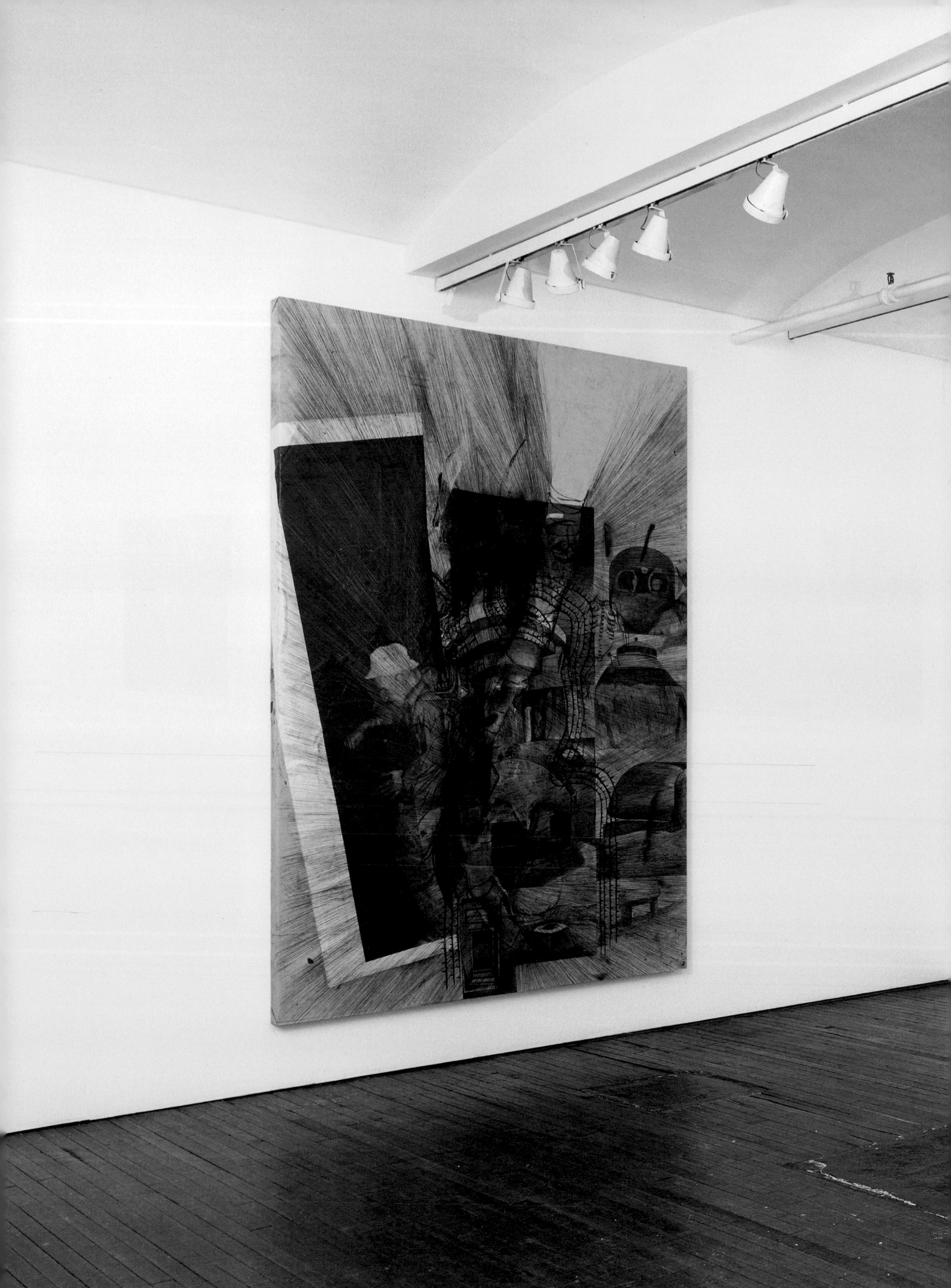

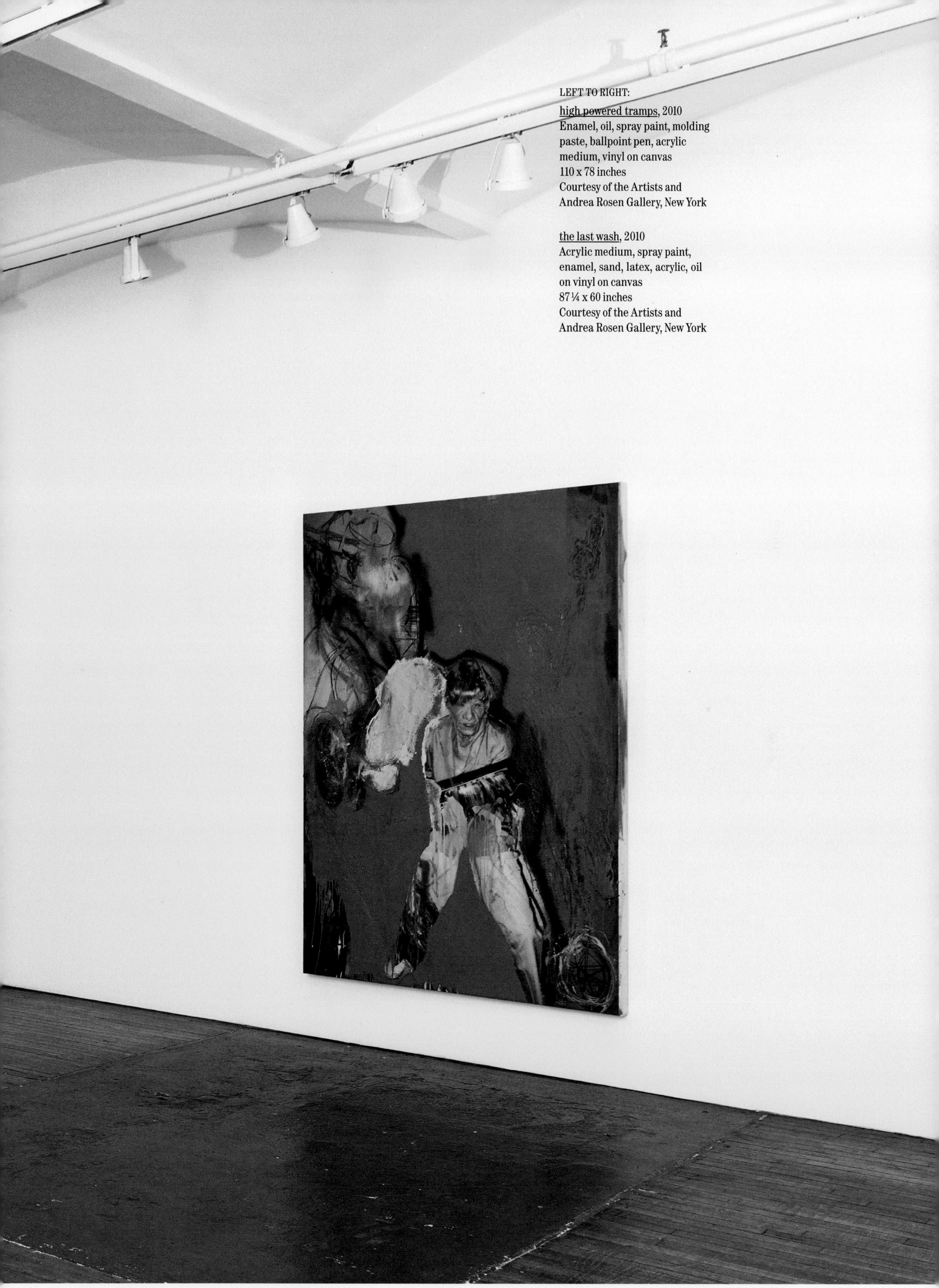

LEFT TO RIGHT:

high powered tramps, 2010
Enamel, oil, spray paint, molding paste, ballpoint pen, acrylic medium, vinyl on canvas
110 x 78 inches
Courtesy of the Artists and Andrea Rosen Gallery, New York

the last wash, 2010
Acrylic medium, spray paint, enamel, sand, latex, acrylic, oil on vinyl on canvas
87 ¼ x 60 inches
Courtesy of the Artists and Andrea Rosen Gallery, New York

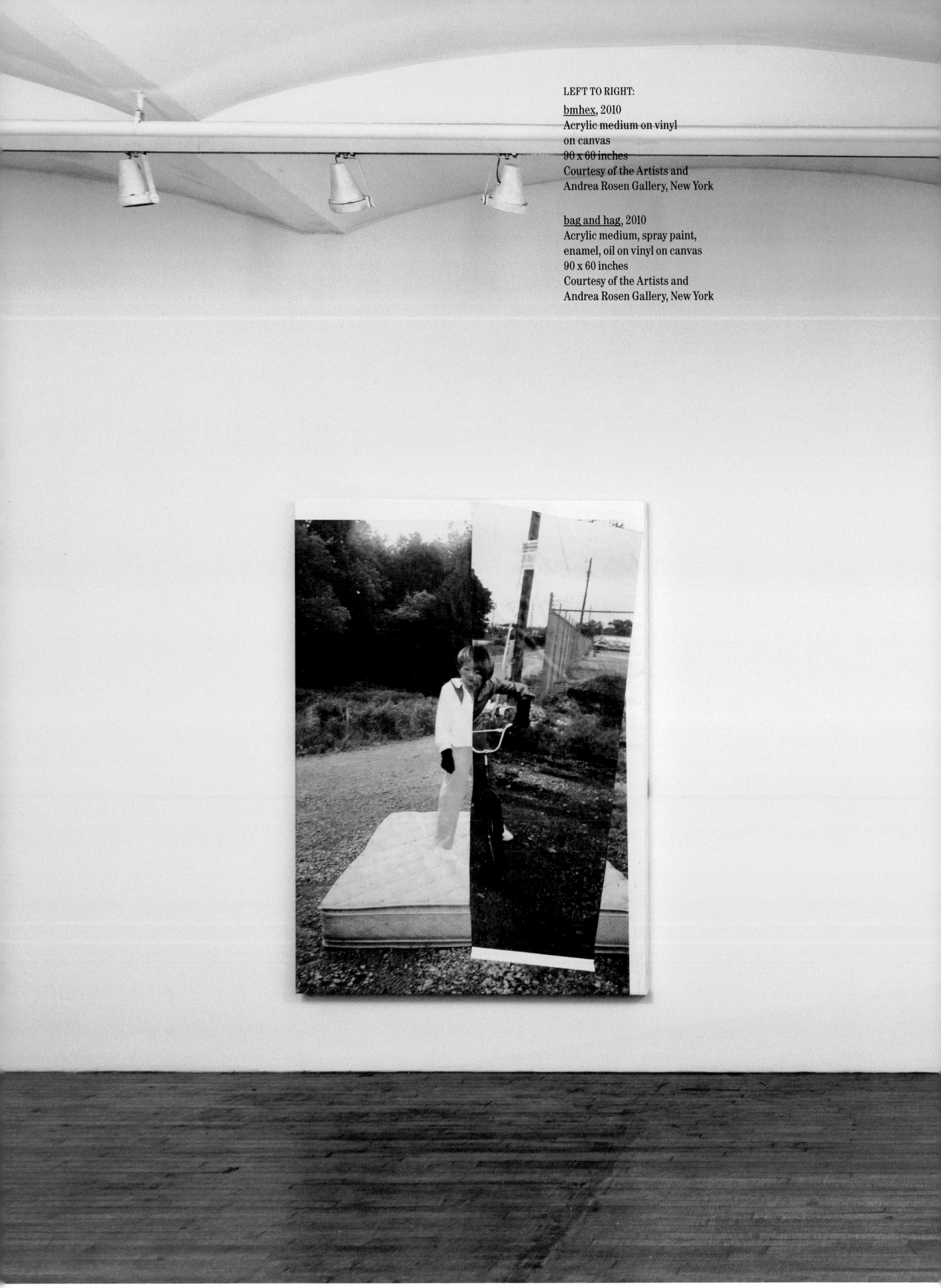

LEFT TO RIGHT:

bmhex, 2010
Acrylic medium on vinyl
on canvas
90 x 60 inches
Courtesy of the Artists and
Andrea Rosen Gallery, New York

bag and hag, 2010
Acrylic medium, spray paint,
enamel, oil on vinyl on canvas
90 x 60 inches
Courtesy of the Artists and
Andrea Rosen Gallery, New York

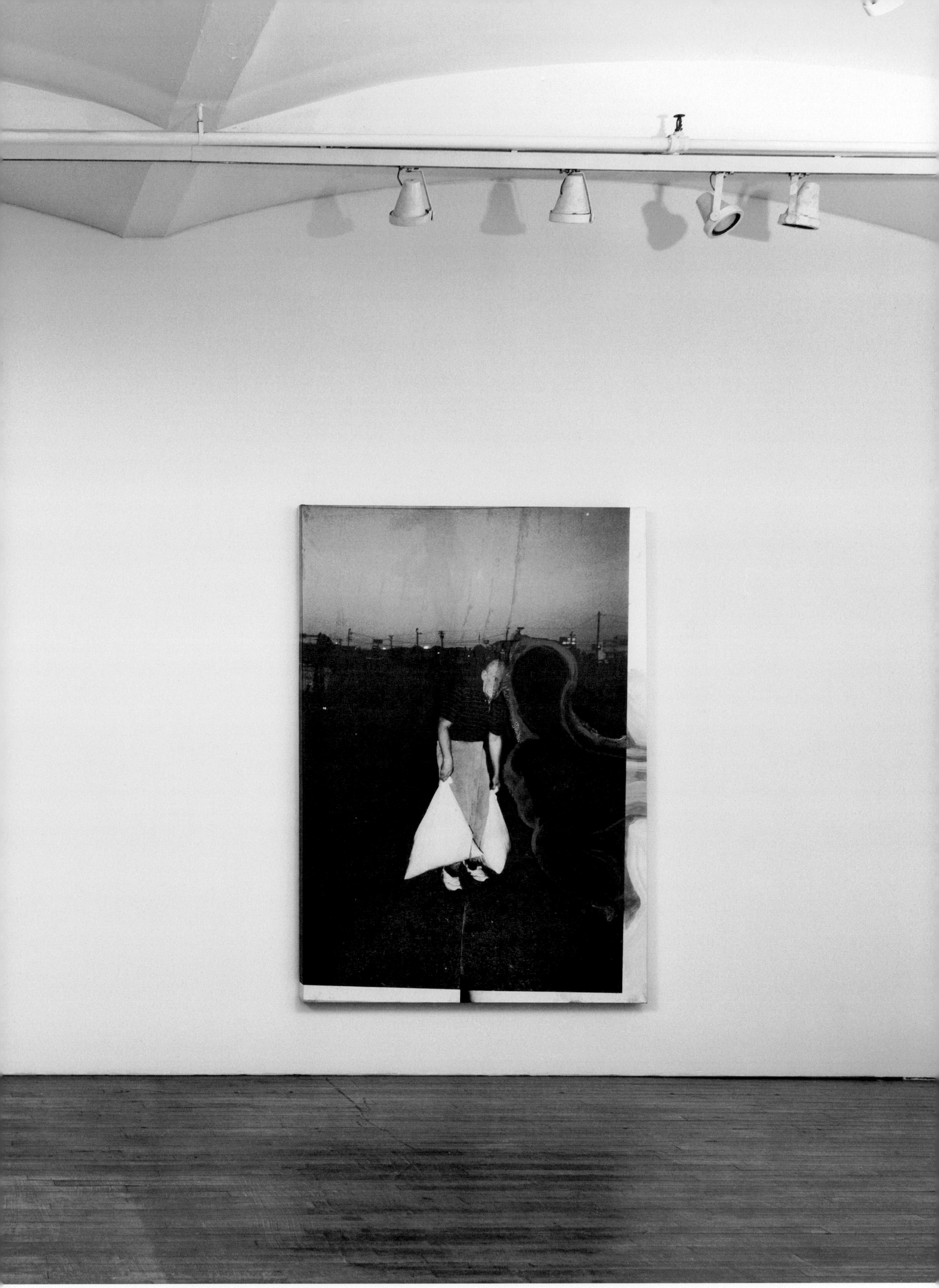

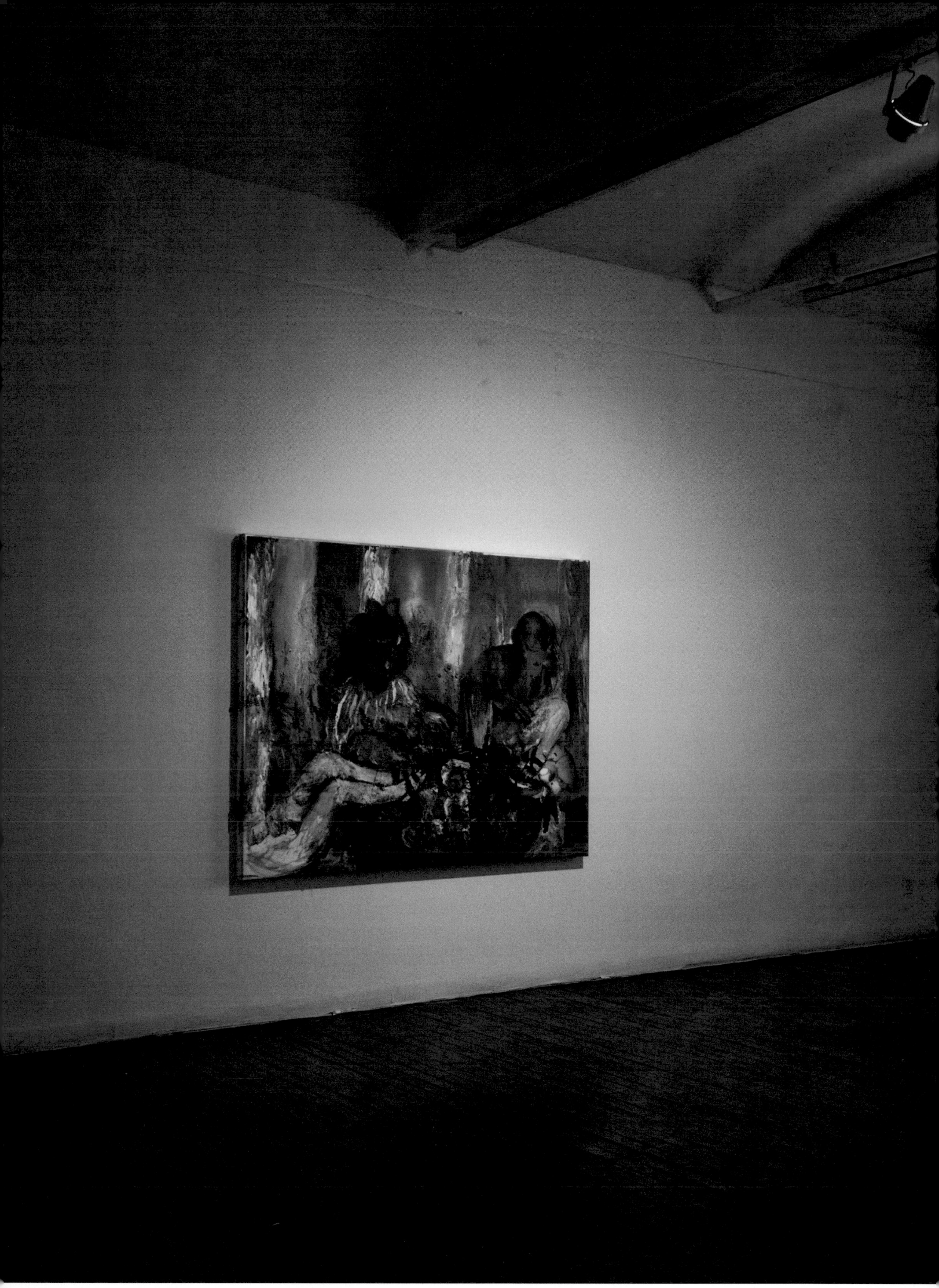

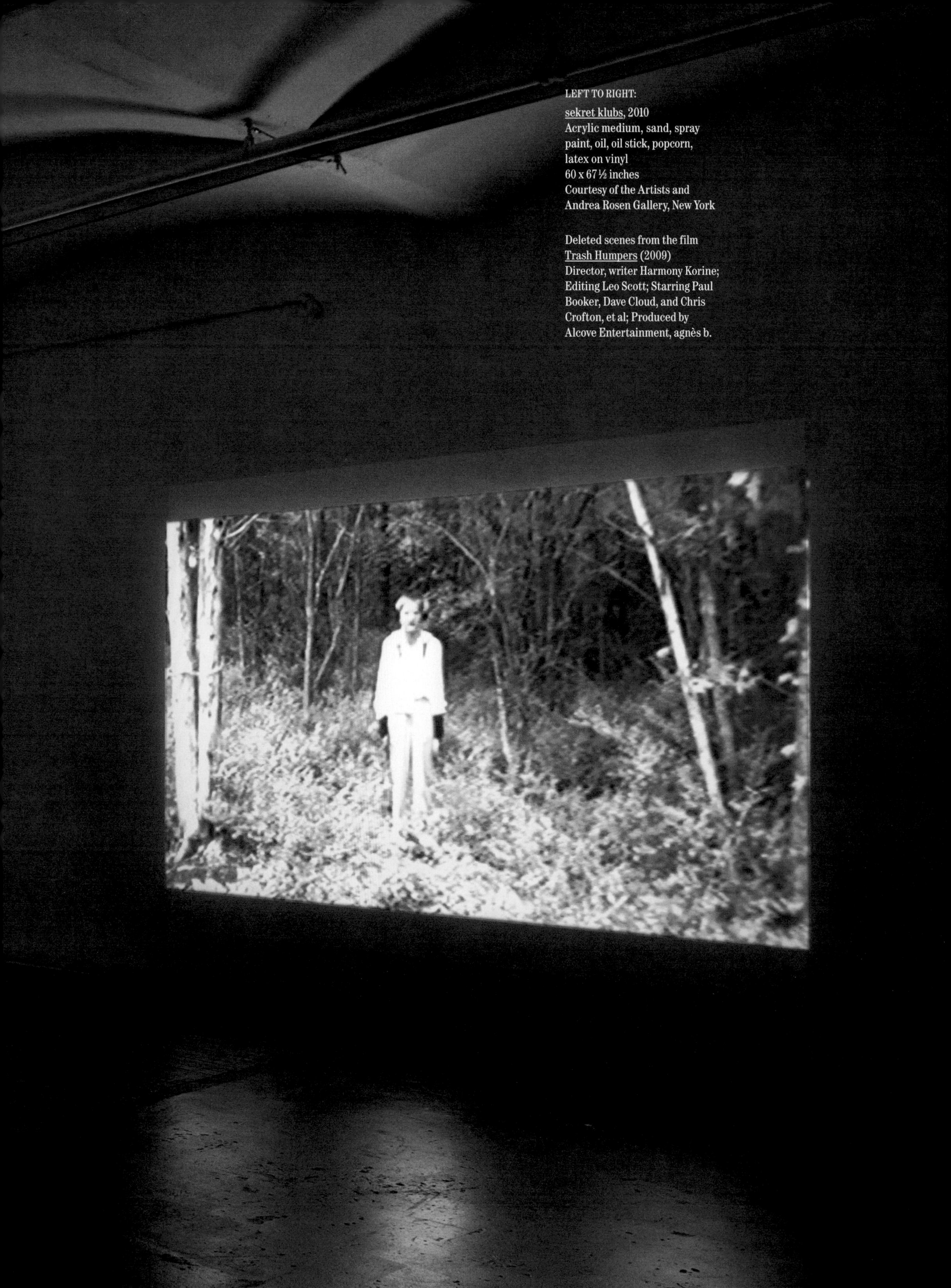

LEFT TO RIGHT:

sekret klubs, 2010
Acrylic medium, sand, spray paint, oil, oil stick, popcorn, latex on vinyl
60 x 67 ½ inches
Courtesy of the Artists and Andrea Rosen Gallery, New York

Deleted scenes from the film Trash Humpers (2009)
Director, writer Harmony Korine; Editing Leo Scott; Starring Paul Booker, Dave Cloud, and Chris Crofton, et al; Produced by Alcove Entertainment, agnès b.

SHADOWFUX

ISBN: 978-2-906496-59-0 (FRANCE) ISBN: 978-1-884692-09-3 (NORTH AMERICA)

PUBLISHED BY THE AGNÈS B. ENDOWMENT FUND AND SWISS INSTITUTE CONTEMPORARY ART